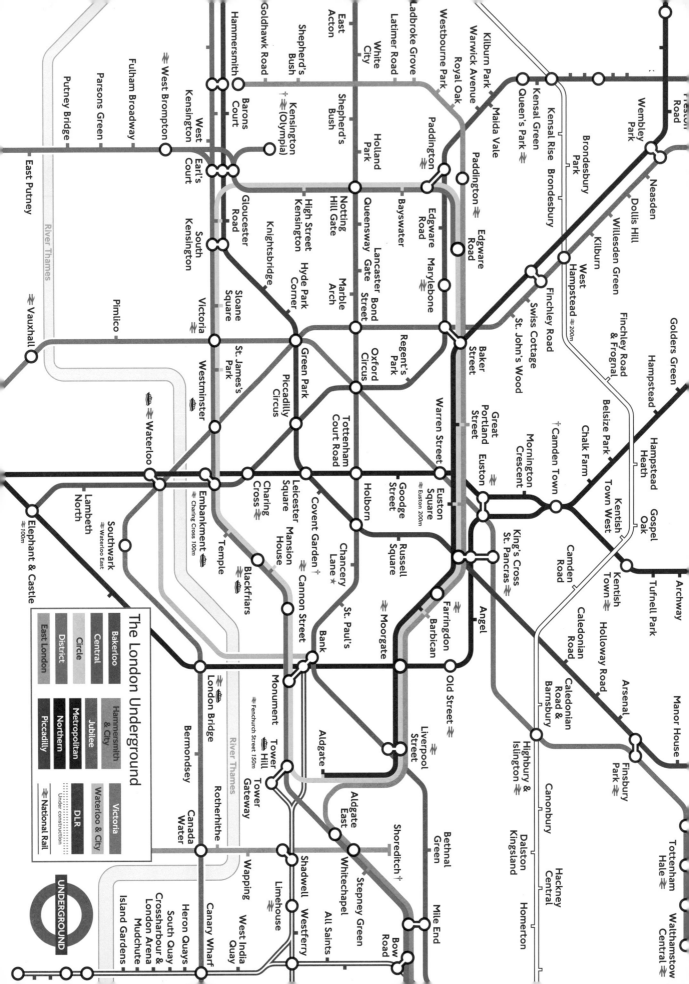

Let's go 3

von Carl Taylor
sowie Wolfgang Hamm
und Elizabeth Daymond

Herausgeber: Dr. Werner Kieweg, M. A.

Ernst Klett Verlag
Stuttgart · Leipzig

Let's go 3

Im Auftrag des Verlags herausgegeben von:
Dr. Werner Kieweg, M.A., Schwabmünchen

Erarbeitet von:
Carl Taylor, M.A., Maidencombe
sowie
Wolfgang Hamm, Marktredwitz, Elizabeth Daymond, M.A., Kiel

Beratung:
Maria Büse-Dallmann, Unna; Thomas Denk, Karlsruhe;
Ute Fritsch, Ulm; Sibylle Olms, Everswinkel; Ingrid Preedy, Dortmund;
Brigitte Seidl, Bochum; Sabine Weingärtner, Schwäbisch Gmünd;
Tanja Wiedmann, Lauffen

Visuelle Gestaltung:
Robert Harvey, London; Christian Dekelver, Weinstadt
sowie
Sven Palmowski, Barcelona

Zusatzmaterialien für Schülerinnen und Schüler zu diesem Band:

Workbook mit Audio-CD und Lernsoftware	978-3-12-582638-0
Workbook mit Audio-CD	978-3-12-582637-3
Workbook Challenge	978-3-12-585867-1
Trainingsheft Kompetenztest Englisch	978-3-12-582652-6
Klasse 7/8 mit Audio-CD	

1. Auflage   1 9 8 7 6 | 2014 13 12 11

Alle Drucke dieser Auflage sind unverändert und können im Unterricht nebeneinander verwendet werden. Die letzte Zahl bezeichnet das Jahr des Druckes.

Redaktion: Ute Erben, William Sears

Herstellung: Peter Strinz
Umschlagfotos: Mauritius (Merten), Mittenwald;
            Avenue Images GmbH (Stockbyte Gold), Hamburg
Reproduktion: Meyle + Müller, Medien-Management, Pforzheim
Druck: Himmer AG, Augsburg
Printed in Germany
ISBN-13: 978-3-12-582631-1

Hello and welcome to *Let's go 3*!

Hi! Remember me? I'm DJ Dan from Galaxy Radio! Welcome back! Before we start, there is some information about your new book. You'll hear some of my programmes in Let's go 3. So see you again soon!

Let's go 3 besteht aus acht Units. Die Units 1, 3, 5 und 7 sind so aufgebaut, wie du es gewohnt bist: Im Abschnitt **Intro** geht es mit dem Thema der Unit los. Dann kommen die Teile **Language** und **Text** mit einigen kürzeren und einem langen Lesetext. Im Inhaltsverzeichnis siehst du, um was es dabei jeweils geht. Im Teil **Practice** wird geübt, und unter **Words** findest du Übungen zu den neuen Wörtern der Unit. Außerdem gibt es hier hilfreiche Tipps zum Umgang mit dem Wörterbuch. In den Teilen **Grammar** und **Let's check** ist noch einmal alles zusammengefasst, was du in der Unit gelernt hast.

Die Units 2, 4, 6 und 8 sind „Kurzunits". Hier gibt es zunächst vier **Topic**-Seiten zum Thema der Unit. Dann folgt unter **Project** eine Projektaufgabe, die du zusammen mit einigen deiner Mitschülerinnen und Mitschüler bearbeiten kannst. Auf der Seite **Let's check** findest du wieder eine Zusammenfassung und außerdem unter **Strategy** viele Tipps zum Training von Hören, Sprechen, Lesen und Schreiben.

Nach den Units 4 und 8 gibt es den Teil **Revision**. Hier kannst du selbstständig üben und wiederholen. Es folgt noch ein Teil **Extra** mit spannenden Infos über Großbritannien und London, Gedichten und Übungen zur Mediation (Vermitteln und Übersetzen).

Wörter, die du nicht mehr weißt, kannst du in der alphabetischen Wortliste ab S. 107 nachschlagen. Danach findest du ganz am Ende eine Liste der unregelmäßigen Verben, die Zahlen, die Lösungen der Revision-Seiten und nützliche Sätze für den Unterricht.

 In den Tipp-Boxen gibt es viele Tipps und Tricks, die das Lernen leichter machen.

Erinnerst du dich noch, was die Zeichen vor Texten und Übungen bedeuten? Hier sind noch einmal die drei wichtigsten:

(◎) Diese Teile gibt es auch auf der Audio-CD im Workbook.

1 Übungen zum Unit-Inhalt

1 Übungen zum Sprechen, Zusammenarbeiten und Selbermachen

Extra

London

a

The Notting Hill Carnival is during the last weekend in August. The first carnival was in 1964. It was just a street party. Today it's a very big event. Over two million people take part every year.

> The Notting Hill Carnival is fun.
> I go every year with my parents.
> You can dance and listen to the music.
> We always watch the processions.

The Tower of London is a very old castle. It was the home of kings and queens for hundreds of years. Buckingham Palace is the Queen's home in London now. Today, tourists can visit the palace and the tower.

The Tower of London

> I've got an uncle in America.
> He stays with us every summer.
> He always wants to see the same sights. It's so boring. How often can you look at Buckingham Palace?

1 London is a great city!

Find out.

1. Why does Terry like the Notting Hill Carnival?
2. Why is it so boring for Sam when his uncle is in London?
3. Why is Emma so excited?
4. Why is shopping in London so awesome for Lisa?

2 Speaking: Interesting sights

Make dialogues with a partner.

A: What would you like to do in London?
B: I'd like to visit the Tower of London.
A: Why?
B: Because I like castles.   ...

It could be fun. I've never seen … .
I like … .   I think … .   ...

The Hindu temple is in North London. It's the largest Hindu temple in Europe. Every year 50,000 people go to Hindu festivals there.

I've got an invitation to an Indian wedding. It's near the Hindu temple. I'm so excited. I'm sure the wedding will be fantastic.

The shops in London are awesome. They've got great clothes. But they're very expensive, so I don't buy things often.

Most tourists go to Oxford Street, in the West End. The most famous shops are there.

3 Listening: A temple 🎧

Some tourists are visiting the Hindu temple. *Listen and take notes.*

1. The temple opened in … .
2. The parts for the temple came from … .
3. People worked for … years to make the temple in London.
4. … schools have visited the temple.
5. … people have visited the temple.

▷ 4 More about London

a) *Make a list of sights in London.*

b) *Find information about one of the sights. You can look in the library or on the internet. Then tell the class.*

– What's the name of the sight?
– Where is it?
– What can you do / see there?

b Sam's uncle, Fred, visits London every summer.
He's sent an e-mail.

Mr Spencer: Can you show Fred the Tower of
London, Sam?
Sam: The Tower of London? Again?
We always do that with Fred.
Mr Spencer: Have you got any good ideas?
Sam: I can show him the London Eye.
Mr Spencer: I think he'll enjoy that.
Sam: Does he like music?
Mr Spencer: Yes, he does.
Sam: I'll take him to the Notting Hill
Carnival, too.
The bands play great music
there. And it's free.
Mr Spencer: When does the carnival start?
Sam: On Sunday. Terry always goes
there. We can meet him.

Say it!

We always **do** that.	*Das **machen** wir immer.*
Terry always **goes** there.	*Terry **geht** immer dorthin.*

5 A visit from America

What's missing?   play   goes   visits   do   likes   wants   starts

1. Fred … London every summer.
2. Sam and Fred always … the same
things.
3. Sam … to go to the London Eye.
4. Fred … music.

5. The bands … great music at the
carnival.
6. The carnival … on Sunday.
7. Terry always … to the carnival.

6 Speaking: Have you got any good ideas?

a) *Think about the places and activities
in your town. Make two lists.*

interesting ☺	boring ☹
leisure centre	park
…	…

b) *Make dialogues with a partner. Use your lists.*

A: My cousin wants to visit me. What can we do?
Have you got any good ideas?
B: You can show her ☹. She'll like that.
A: That's boring. We always do that.
B: Well, you could show her ☺.
A: That's a good idea.

That's cool.
He'll/She'll enjoy that.
…

That's awful.
I hate that.
…

c Lisa is at home. She's got her mobile phone.

Lisa: Hello?

Emma: Hi, Lisa, it's Emma. Would you like to come to the wedding on Saturday? We can go together.

Lisa: That's so cool. I've never seen a Hindu wedding. Can I wear my new sweatshirt?

Emma: No, you can't. We ought to wear Indian clothes. I can give you some.

Lisa: Thanks. Is the wedding in the temple?

Emma: No, it isn't. There aren't any weddings in the temple. But it's near the temple. We must leave my house at nine o'clock. We mustn't be late. And we ought to visit the temple, too.

Lisa: OK.

Say it!

We **ought to wear** Indian clothes.

*Wir **sollten eigentlich** indische Kleidung **tragen**.*

7 An Indian wedding

Make sentences.

| can't wear | mustn't be | ought to visit | can go | can give | ought to wear | must leave |

1. Lisa and Emma/to the wedding
   Lisa and Emma can go to the wedding.
2. Lisa/her new sweatshirt
   Lisa can't … .   *Go on, please.*

3. Lisa and Emma/Indian clothes
4. Emma/Lisa some clothes
5. They/Emma's house at nine o'clock
6. They/late for the wedding
7. The girls/the Hindu temple

8 Speaking: Special clothes

1

come to a wedding /
Saturday

2

play in a football game /
tomorrow

3

help me in the garden /
Sunday

Make dialogues with a partner.

1. *A:* Hi, would you like to come to a wedding on Saturday?
   B: That's cool.
   A: You ought to wear your best clothes.
   B: OK. I've got … .
2. *Go on, please.*

your best clothes
a red T-shirt
old clothes/jeans
a nice shirt/dress
…

Let's go to the carnival! ◎

It was the last weekend in August. Sam and his uncle were at the London Eye. Now Uncle Fred wanted to visit the Tower of London and then Buckingham Palace. 5

"We go there every year," said Sam. "I love it," said Fred. "We haven't got a Queen in America."
"My friend Terry is at the Notting Hill Carnival. We should go there. 10 It'll be fun. People dance and play music. You can eat West Indian food."
"OK," said Fred. "We can go to the Tower of London tomorrow."

15 Sam decided to take the Underground to Oxford Circus and change to the Central Line. There were lots of people on the train. The train left the station and went into a tunnel. Then it stopped.

"What's the problem?" asked Fred.
"This often happens," said Sam.
20 But then suddenly it was very dark.
"What do we do now?" asked Fred.
"How long will we be here?"
"I don't know," said Sam.
Sam took his mobile phone. "Look.
25 I can use my phone like a torch."
Other people took their mobile phones. They used them like torches in the dark train.
They waited and waited. It was now
30 very hot.

Then suddenly the train started and they came out of the tunnel.
They came to the next station. The doors opened. A voice said loudly, "Please get off the train. There is a problem in the tunnel."
Sam and his uncle came out of the Underground station.
35 "That was awful," said Fred. "Let's take a taxi. I don't want to sit in another dark tunnel."

Fred saw a black London taxi. He opened the door and they jumped in.
"Notting Hill Gate, please," said Sam.
"You can't drive there today," said the driver. "It's the carnival."
40 They climbed out of the taxi.
"Uncle Fred, quick," said Sam. "A bus is coming. It goes to Notting Hill Gate."
Sam and Fred jumped into the bus. They bought two tickets. The bus went slowly along the road.

"I think we'll go to Piccadilly Circus," said Sam. "And along Oxford Street."
45 Fred looked at the sights. But suddenly the bus stopped.
"What's happening now?" asked Fred.
Sam went to the driver. When he came back, he said, "There's a demonstration near Trafalgar Square."
"OK," said Fred. "That's that. Let's walk. Have you got a map?"
50 "Yes," said Sam.
"May I see it?"
They got off the bus and started to walk.

After one hour, they arrived in Notting Hill. They heard music and saw dancers
55 in the streets.
"Does Terry know that we want to meet him?" asked Fred. "You ought to phone him."
"OK." Sam took his mobile phone.
60 "Oh, no," he said. "I've got no credit."
"This is crazy," said Fred. "Haven't you got a meeting place?"
Then Sam's phone rang. It was Terry.
"Hi, Terry," said Sam. "Yes, we're in
65 front of the Café Mambo. Where are you?"
Then Fred heard Terry's voice.
"I'm behind you, Sam," said Terry.
"You don't need your phone."

1 Where were Sam and Fred?

What's the right order?

| In the taxi | In Notting Hill | On the bus |

| In front on the café | On the Underground | At the London Eye |

1. 'At the London Eye' is first.
2. ... . *Go on, please.*

2 Fred's story

Fred sent an e-mail to a friend in America. *What did he say?*

```
Dear Charles,
I was in London with Sam yesterday. First we went to the
London Eye. That was really interesting. Then we decided
to go to the Notting Hill Carnival.
First we took the ... . But then it stopped. ...
```

1 An interesting job

In the summer Louise works in the Tower of London. *Talk about her day.*

1

go to work / by Underground

2

start work / 9.30

3

talk to tourists / about the tower

4

tell stories / about kings and queens

5

finish work / 5.30

6

arrive home / 7.00

1. Louise goes to work by Underground.   2. She starts … .   *Go on, please.*

2 A trip to London

You want to book a trip to London. *What's the right question?*

1. *Du möchtest wissen, wie viel ein Flug nach London kostet.*
   a) How much does a flight to London cost?
   b) How many planes go to London?
2. *Du möchtest die Abflugszeit wissen.*
   a) Where does the plane leave?
   b) When does the plane leave?
3. *Du möchtest wissen, wo das Flugzeug landet.*
   a) When does the plane land?
   b) Where does the plane land?
4. *Du möchtest wissen, wie du in die Innenstadt kommst.*
   a) How do we go from the airport to London?
   b) How do we go from London to the airport?
5. *Du möchtest wissen, wie viel ein U-Bahn-Ticket kostet.*
   a) Where can I get an Underground ticket?
   b) How much does an Underground ticket cost?
6. *Du möchtest jemanden fragen, ob es billige Hotels gibt.*
   a) Do you know any cheap hotels?
   b) How much is the cheapest hotel?

3 Listening: London can be cheap!

A German family is at a London Tourist Information Centre. They think London is expensive. The woman is telling them about some free activities.
Listen and make a list of free activities.

Free activities in London

the British Museum
the …

4 Carnival tips

Match the parts of the sentences.

1. All the roads in Notting Hill are closed on the day of the carnival. You mustn't
2. You ought to
3. It's difficult to meet friends without a mobile phone. You ought to
4. West Indian food is great! You ought to
5. Remember, it's summer! You must
6. You must be careful

drink lots of water.
try some at the carnival.
with wallets and money at the carnival.
drive.
take one.
take the Underground to Notting Hill.

5 Speaking: On the Underground

You're at Paddington Station and you want to go to one of the places in this unit.
Look at the Underground map at the front of the book. Make dialogues with a partner.

A: I'd like to see Big Ben. How can we go there?
B: We can take the Circle Line from here to Baker Street. Then we change to the Jubilee Line. We get off at Westminster.

Place	Underground
1. Big Ben	Westminster
2. Buckingham Palace	Green Park
3. Trafalgar Square	Charing Cross
4. Science Museum	South Kensington
5. Tower of London	Tower Hill

6 Mediation: The London Eye

You're in London with your class. You're at the London Eye. Two German people want to book a trip on the Eye.
Can you help them?

Woman:	Good morning. What can I do for you?
Mr Fiebig:	Sage, dass wir gerne Fahrkarten für das ‚London Eye' kaufen wollen.
You:	These people would like to …
Woman:	I'm sorry, they must wait for two hours. I haven't got any tickets now.
You:	…
Mrs Fiebig:	Können wir Karten für morgen kaufen?
You:	…
Woman:	Yes. The first trip is at half past nine. Tickets are £12.
You:	…
Mr Fiebig:	Können wir bitte zwei Karten für morgen früh haben?
You:	…
Woman:	Yes, they can. That's £24, please.
You:	…

TIPP

Arbeiten mit dem Wörterbuch I

Wenn du etwas auf Englisch nicht sagen kannst, weil dir ein Wort fehlt, dann kannst du im **deutsch-englischen** Teil deines Wörterbuchs nachschauen, z. B.

Is there a "Jugendherberge" near here?

Jugendherberge youth hostel
jugendlich ❶ (*jung*) young
❷ (*jung wirkend*) youthful

Wenn du die deutsche Bedeutung eines englischen Wortes nicht weißt, dann schaust du im **englisch-deutschen** Teil deines Wörterbuchs nach, z. B.

We've got lots of <u>youth hostels</u> here in Britain.

youth hostel Jugendherberge
you've [ju:v] *Kurzform von* **you have**
Yu·go·sla·via [ˈjuːgəʊˈslɑːvɪə] Jugoslawien

In einem Wörterbuch sind Wörter nicht nur nach ihren Anfangsbuchstaben geordnet, sondern auch nach den nachfolgenden Buchstaben, z. B.
a<u>b</u>out – a<u>c</u>cident – a<u>d</u>dress – ad<u>v</u>enture – a<u>f</u>ter

1. In welcher Reihenfolge stehen die folgenden Wörter im Wörterbuch? Schreibe die Lösung auf ein Blatt Papier.
   street – bus – famous – temple – wedding – Underground – change – unit
2. Und in welcher Reihenfolge findest du die folgenden Wörter? Schreibe die Lösung ebenfalls auf ein Blatt Papier.
   sweatshirt – sea – sad – skateboard – smelly – strange – suddenly – spicy
3. Schreibe nun einige Wörter aus dem Wörterbuch heraus, verändere ihre Reihenfolge und lege sie dann deinem Partner zur Lösung vor.

7 Word web: In a big city

a) *Make a word web for 'in a big city' in your exercise book. You can also use a dictionary.*

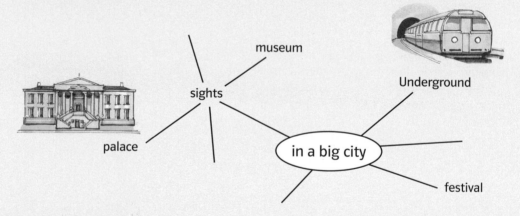

b) *Which things in the word web have you got in your city, town or village?*

My town has got a … but there isn't a … . We've got … .
Go on, please.

▷ 8 Listen and speak 💿

[i:]

1. Speak to me! Is it a secret?
2. Does he meet Lisa at the beach?
3. It's three metres from the tree to the sea.
4. These football teams eat cheap pizzas
   on Monday evening.

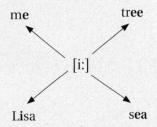

There are 17 words in these sentences where you say [i:].
Find them and make four lists in your exercise book.

9 Word friends

Which words go together?

1. 'street' and 'party' make
   'street party'.
2. 'taxi' ... .
   Go on, please.

street	Underground	Palace	Circus
taxi	Buckingham	station	place
Piccadilly	mobile	driver	team
Hindu	Monday	party	phone
football	meeting	evening	temple

10 One word is wrong!

1. temple, palace, church, attic.
   'attic' is wrong.
2. Germany, Europe, England, Italy
   Go on, please.

3. king, father, mother, uncle
4. comic, book, pencil, magazine
5. Underground, taxi, plane, bus
6. late, week, month, year

11 Word puzzles

a) *What's the word?*

1. Kings and queens live in a ... .
   – That's a palace.
2. Your father's brother is your ... .
   Go on, please.
3. A train leaves and arrives at a ... .
4. When people leave one Underground
   train and go to another, they ... .
5. Hindu people don't go to a church,
   they go to a ... .
6. When two people marry there's a ... .
7. You can see processions and hear
   music at a ... .

▷ b) *Make more word puzzles for a partner.*

12 A cartoon

London's changed since our last visit!

change – *sich verändern*; since – *seit*

Present simple *(einfache Gegenwart)*

Verwendung:
Du verwendest das present simple, *um über etwas zu sprechen, das regelmäßig oder oft stattfindet.*

I **play** football **every Tuesday**.
He **visits** his grandma **very often**.

Bildung:
* *Verneinung und Fragen werden mit* do *gebildet.*
* *He, she, it, das „s" muss mit!*

I **don't go** to the cinema very often.
How often **do** you **go** to the cinema?
She **goes** to school by bike.
He always **takes** the bus.
It **leaves** in front of his house.

Achtung!
Wenn etwas gerade eben geschieht, wird das present progressive *verwendet.*

I'm sorry, you**'re wearing** the wrong trousers.
But I **wear** these trousers every day!

Welche Beispielsätze passen zu Cartoon A? Warum?

Ought to, must, mustn't

Du verwendest ought to, *um zu sagen, was man eigentlich tun sollte.*

You **ought to** go to work by train, Dad!

Du verwendest must, *um zu sagen, was man tun muss.*

But you **must** buy a ticket.

Du verwendest mustn't, *um zu sagen, was man nicht tun darf.*

You **mustn't** get on the train without a ticket.

Welcher der Beispielsätze passt zu Cartoon B? Warum?

Checklist

Ich kann	
… sagen, wohin ich gerne gehen würde.	I'd like to visit the Notting Hill Carnival.
… sagen, dass ich etwas langweilig finde.	Buckingham Palace is so boring.
… sagen, dass ich etwas toll finde.	The shops in London are awesome.
… sagen, dass etwas regelmäßig geschieht.	He stays with us every summer.
… sagen, dass etwas immer das Gleiche ist.	We always go there.
… sagen, was man eigentlich machen sollte.	We ought to wear Indian clothes.
… sagen, was ich machen muss.	I must leave the house at nine o'clock.
… sagen, was nicht passieren darf.	We mustn't be late.

Checkout: The two camels

One day, a young camel was talking to his father.
"Dad, why do we have humps?" he asked.
"Well, the humps contain fat. That's our food for the many days when we're in the desert."
"Thanks," said the youngster. Then he asked, "Dad, why do we have long eyelashes?"
"Well, son," said the father, "in the desert there are sandstorms with lots of sand. We need long eyelashes to protect our eyes."
"OK. And why do we have such big feet?"
"Well, son, the sand is very soft in the desert. Our big feet stop us sinking into the sand."
"Well thanks, Dad," said the youngster. "So what the heck are we doing in London Zoo?"

Hast du die Geschichte verstanden? Wo leben die Kamele?
Hier gibt es wieder einige Wörter und Wendungen, die du nicht kennst. Du kannst sie aus dem Zusammenhang erschließen oder in der alphabetischen Wortliste ab Seite 107 nachschlagen.

TIPP

Tipps: The two camels
1. was talking: *Das ist die Vergangenheitsform von* is talking.
2. humps, eyelashes: *Diese Körperteile siehst du auf dem Bild.*
3. sandstorm, sinking: *Diese Wörter sind im Deutschen ganz ähnlich.*

It's good to talk!

Hello?

Sarah, is that you? It's me, Linda.

Ben? It's Barbara. Can we talk?

Where are you?

	Text and talk	Chatterbox
UK phone numbers:		
during the day	30p per minute	20p per minute
evening/weekend	10p per minute	5p per minute
Mobiles in the same network:		
during the day	30p per minute	25p per minute
evening/weekend	10p per minute	5p per minute
Text messages:	15p per message	30p per message
Photo messages:	20p per message	35p per message

Lots of people have got mobile phones, but phone calls aren't always cheap. There are lots of different plans, but phone bills can still be a problem, and some people can't pay them.

Click to download the coolest ring tones

1 Phones and plans

a) *Make a list of phone words on these two pages. Add new words to your list as you work through the unit.*

b) *Which plan could be best for you? Say why.*

2 Speaking: On the phone

Act short phone dialogues with a partner. Partner A phones, partner B answers.

Partner A

You can ask …
where your partner is.
can he/she talk?
can you meet?
…

Partner B

You can say …
where you are.
that you can talk/can't talk because … .
where and when you can meet.
…

Remember:
Start and finish the dialogue nicely.
You can also use your own ideas.

3 Speaking: Have you got a mobile phone?

a) *Make a survey. Write your partners' answers.*

	Yes	No
Have you got a mobile phone?	...	...
Do you always take your mobile phone with you?	...	
Do you sleep with your mobile phone near your bed?	...	
Do you pay your own phone bills?	...	
Do you download ring tones?	...	
Do you send text messages?	...	
Did you get your mobile phone more than a year ago?	...	
...	...	

b) *Talk about your results.*

   ... people have got a mobile phone. ... people always ... . *Go on, please.*

b Mobile phone tips

Not everybody wants to listen when you talk on your mobile phone!
Mobile phones can also be dangerous sometimes.
Here are some tips.

1. Switch off your phone in the cinema, a restaurant, the classroom, or the church. Some people are angry when a phone rings in a quiet place.
2. Talk quietly. You don't have to shout. Your friend will hear you.
3. When you have to call somebody, think. Who is sitting behind you? Do they want to hear your problems?
4. Don't use your phone when you're walking along the road, or when you're on a bike or a skateboard! It's dangerous.
5. Be careful with your phone. Somebody could steal it!

Say it!

Talk quietly.	*Sprich leise.*
Switch off your phone in the cinema.	*Schalte dein Handy im Kino aus.*

4 The tips

a) *Which tip goes with which picture?*

1. Picture number … goes with tip … .
2. *Go on, please.*

▷ b) *Talk about the tips with a partner. Are they good tips for you and your friends?*

Sometimes people ….   That's awful.

I always …./ I never ….   I don't think that's a problem.

5 Speaking: What do you think?

Look what these people are saying.
Are they right?

A: Do you think Number 1 is right?
B: No, I don't. I think he's wrong.
A: Why do you think he's wrong?
B: Because …

1

Nobody under 18 should have a mobile phone.

2

Every boy and girl should have a mobile phone.

3

Mobile phones should be free for young children.

4

People should switch off their mobile phones on trains.

6 Listening with DJ Dan: In Devon

DJ Dan is talking about mobile phones today. *What's the right answer?*

1. Tim stayed
   a) on a campsite.
   b) in a hotel.

2. One afternoon the boys
   a) went swimming.
   b) walked along the beach.

3. They didn't go back because
   a) they couldn't swim.
   b) it was too dangerous.

4. Tim phoned his parents and
   a) they were angry.
   b) a boat came to get the boys.

7 Writing: A mobile phone story

Did a mobile phone help you or a friend? Or did somebody use a mobile phone and you hated it? *Write about it.* *Find an ending for the story.*

When did it happen? • Where did it happen?
Who was with you? • What happened?

8 A song: Why didn't you call me?

Gray, Macy/Ruzumna, Jeremy

We went out one night,
Everything went right.
We got something started,
It was outta sight.
We had such a good time,
Hey! Why didn't you call me?

I thought I'd see you again.
By the phone I wait,
Staring into space.
Thinking about our first kiss
Out on our first date.

everything – *alles*; we got something started – *wir haben etwas miteinander angefangen*; outta sight – *toll*; by – *neben*; staring into space – *ins Leere starrend*; kiss – *Kuss*; date – *Verabredung*

Project: Communication

There are many ways to send messages and talk with other people. *Work in groups and do a project about communication. You can do project A or project B.*

A
Look at the history of communication. How did people send messages 100 or 200 years ago?

B
Think about the future of communication. How will people send messages in 50 or 100 years?

You can show your work to the class in ONE of two ways:

an **exhibition**
with posters and texts

a **presentation**
in English

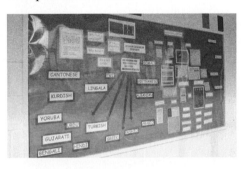

Exhibition
1. Find texts and pictures for your exhibition.
2. Put the pictures and texts into groups. The exhibition should tell a story.
3. Make posters with the pictures and texts. There should be one poster for every part of the story.
4. The pictures shouldn't be too small and the texts must be easy to read. Maybe you can use a computer.
5. What do people in the class think of the exhibition? Make a worksheet for them. Then they can tell you.

Presentation
1. There should be pictures and short texts in your presentation.
2. Put the pictures and short texts into groups. The presentation should tell a story.
3. Make notes on cards. You should say something about every picture and short text.
4. More than one person should do the presentation. That will make it more interesting!
5. Are there any questions at the end of the presentation? Ask the people in the class!

Checklist

Ich kann	
…jemanden fragen, ob er ein Handy besitzt.	Have you got a mobile phone?
…ein Telefongespräch beginnen.	Sarah, is that you? It's me, Linda.
…ein Telefongespräch beenden.	Speak to you later. Bye!
…sagen, dass jemand Recht hat.	I think she's right.
…sagen, dass jemand nicht Recht hat.	I think she's wrong.
…sagen, was jeder haben sollte.	Everybody should have a mobile phone.
…sagen, dass jemand sein Handy ausschalten soll.	Can you switch off your mobile phone, please?

U1 London
U2 Handy
U3 Wales
U4 Schule
U5 Schottland
U6 Musik
U7 Wetter
U8 Sport

Strategy: Reading

Mobile phones: Who pays the bill?
Soon half of all young people in America will have a mobile phone. Many young people say they can't live without a phone. But mobile phones aren't cheap. Somebody must pay the bills.
Dan Brown is thirteen. Last month his parents got a phone bill for $500. Many young people don't understand their mobile phone plan and it's often more expensive than they think.

Too many mobiles?
Francesca lives in Italy. She is addicted to her mobile phones. She has 9 of them, so she always has reception. She sometimes sends 200 text messages in one day. "When you get lots of messages, your friends think you are really cool," she says.
Lots of teenagers in Italy have Francesca's problem. They are addicted to their mobile phones.

Mit der richtigen Taktik ist Lesen gar nicht so schwer. Erarbeite dir diese zwei Zeitungsausschnitte in drei Schritten.

A Vor dem Lesen
Lies zuerst die Überschrift und überlege:

- *Was könnte alles in dem Text stehen?*
- *Was weiß ich schon über dieses Thema?*
- *Was würde mich noch interessieren?*

So bringst du dein Gehirn in die richtige Stimmung!

B Während des Lesens
Lies den Text nun still für dich. Wichtig dabei ist:

- *Du musst nicht jedes Wort gleich verstehen! Lies erst in Ruhe bis zum Ende.*
- *Frage dich, wie viel du verstanden hast. Alles? Die Hälfte? Gar nichts?*
- *Gehe zurück und lies schwierige Stellen noch einmal. Schreibe dir aus jedem Text 2-3 Wörter heraus, die dir am wichtigsten erscheinen.*

C Nach dem Lesen
Arbeite jetzt mit einem Partner zusammen.

- *Erzählt euch gegenseitig, was in den Texten steht und besprecht Stellen, die ihr nicht verstanden habt.*
- *Erschließt euch unbekannte Wörter aus dem Zusammenhang oder schlagt sie im Wörterbuch nach.*

Wales

a Katja's town is twinned with Abergavenny, a town in Wales. Katja plays the trombone. She's in Abergavenny with a band from her town. She's there on an exchange.

Hallo!
Wir sind in Abergavenny
angekommen. Ich wohne bei
einer netten Familie.
Sie haben eine Tochter,
Kerry.
Wales ist schön! Aber
manche Leute hier haben
eine total eigene Sprache.
Sie sprechen Walisisch.
Kein Witz! Ich verstehe
wirklich kein Wort.
Sie sprechen aber
natürlich auch Englisch.

Snowdon ▲

ENGLAND

WALES

Carmarthen

Abergavenny

Swansea

Cardiff

Wales isn't England!

Croeso i Gymru
Welcome to Wales

Every boy and girl in Wales must learn the Welsh language at school.

1 A German girl and a Welsh boy

a) *Say in English what Katja writes in her e-mail.*

Katja has arrived in … .
She's staying … .   *Go on, please.*

b) *Now tell the class about Rhodri in German.*

Rhodri wohnt in Abergavenny.
Er spricht … .   *Go on, please.*

2 Speaking: An exchange visit

A Welsh or English exchange pupil is staying at your house.
Make dialogues with a partner.

> put my clothes here?   use your computer?
> watch TV?   phone my parents?   …

A: This is your room.
B: Great. Can I …?
A: Yes, of course.
B: Can I …?
A: I'm not sure. I'll ask my parents.

There are three million people in Wales – and ten million sheep.

My name is Rhodri Jones. I live in Abergavenny. It's in the south of Wales. I speak English and Welsh. I play football for my town. One day I'd like to play for Manchester United. Maybe I can play for Wales. Then I can play against England and win!

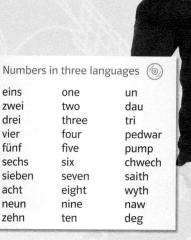

There were lots of coal mines in Wales. Today some are museums.

Numbers in three languages

eins	one	un
zwei	two	dau
drei	three	tri
vier	four	pedwar
fünf	five	pump
sechs	six	chwech
sieben	seven	saith
acht	eight	wyth
neun	nine	naw
zehn	ten	deg

3 Listening: Katja and Kerry

a) Katja is in Kerry's room. They're listening to music. *Right or wrong?*

1. Katja likes the band.
2. Some Welsh bands sing in Welsh.
3. Kerry speaks Welsh like she speaks English.
4. English is older than Welsh.
5. Katja met a boy yesterday evening.
6. Katja doesn't like the boy.

b) *What do you think "Dw i'n dy garu di." means?*

4 More about Wales

Find more information about Wales. Here are some ideas.

What are the biggest towns in Wales?
What other sports do people play in Wales?
What can tourists do there?

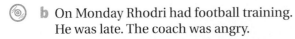

b On Monday Rhodri had football training. He was late. The coach was angry.

Say it!

Where **were** you?	Wo **warst** du?
Did you **forget** the training?	**Hast** du das Training **vergessen**?

5   What happened?

What's missing?

1. Rhodri ... to a concert last night.
2. He ... a German girl there.
3. She ... the trombone in a band.
4. Rhodri ... her again this afternoon.
5. They ... to a café.
6. Rhodri ... the training.

6   Speaking: **Sorry I'm late!**

a) *Act the dialogue.*

    A: Sorry I'm late!
    B: Where were you?
    A: I was in town .
    B: Did you forget the party ?
    A: No, I didn't. I'm sorry!

b) *Make new dialogues with a partner.*

Why were you late? ...	at the swimming pool at school at the shops ...	the football game the audition the meeting ...

c On Wednesday Katja went to the coal mine museum Big Pit. Kerry went with her.

"I don't want to go down the coal mine," said Katja. "Can I stay in the cafeteria?"
"Come on, you'll really like it," said Kerry. "A miner will go with us. My grandad worked here. It was a dangerous job."
"I don't want to go now," said Katja. "I'm waiting for a phone call."
Katja looked at her mobile phone quickly.
"I've got a text message," she said. She read the message carefully. It was from Rhodri.

> Don't forget the football game on Saturday.
> Will you be at the party tonight?

"OK," Katja said happily. "Let's go down the mine now."

Say it!
The job was **dangerous**.
*Die Arbeit war **gefährlich**.*
Katja read the message **carefully**.
*Katja las die Mitteilung **sorgfältig**.*

7 An important message

Match the parts of the sentences.

1. Katja went to a coal mine
2. She wanted to stay
3. She looked
4. She was happy
5. "It's from Rhodri,"
6. He wanted to see her at the party

in the evening.
she said happily.
when she read the message.
in the cafeteria.
at her phone quickly.
on Wednesday.

8 Speaking: Let's meet!

You want to do something with a friend at the weekend.

Act dialogues with a partner.

A: Let's go to the school play.
B: I don't want to go there.
A: Come on, you'll really enjoy it.
B: OK. Where do you want to meet?
A: Let's meet outside the library after school.
B: OK. I'll go with you.

Let's go	Let's meet	When?
to the school play	in the cafeteria	at 6 o'clock
to the museum	in the library	on Saturday morning
to Burger Bar	at the station	at 12 o'clock
to Karen's party	at my house	in half an hour
to the leisure centre	in town	after school

Look at pages 26-29 again. What do you know about Katja and Rhodri?
Now look at the pictures here. What do you think will happen in the story?

Katja and Rhodri

Rhodri and Katja were in a café.
It was Friday afternoon.
"I really want to come to the football game tomorrow," said Katja.
"You know that. But I can't." 5
"It's OK. It's not a problem," said Rhodri. But he wasn't happy.
He liked Katja and he knew that she liked him.
Their problem was the next day. 10
Saturday was the German group's last day in Wales.
"We're going to visit Carmarthen Castle," said Katja quietly.
"Then I must play in a concert in 15
Carmarthen in the evening. It'll be a long day, and the concert is really important."
Rhodri didn't say anything.

20 "I must play in the concert," Katja said again. "This isn't just a holiday. I'm here with the band."
"But the football game is important, too," said Rhodri. Then he looked at
25 her. "It's OK. I understand."
But Katja wasn't so sure. Did he really understand?
'Maybe he thinks that I don't like him,' she thought.
30 Suddenly she said, "Why don't you come with us? We're a big group.
We've got two buses."
"I can't," he said. Then he looked at his watch. "Oh, no. I'll be late for training
35 again."
He looked at Katja. "Are you sure you can't stay here tomorrow? You can watch our football game. Then we can go into town. What do you think?"

40 Katja didn't say anything. She needed a good idea now. She wanted to see

Rhodri again before she went back to Germany, but she was also part of a band. She really wanted to play in the concert. And she didn't want any 45
problems with the group.
"No, I can't," she said. "I'm sorry."
"Then I won't see you again?" asked Rhodri.
Katja tried to laugh. "Maybe your 50
football team will come to Germany.
You can see me then."
Rhodri looked at his watch. "I must go. I'm late."
He ran quickly out of the café. 55

When Katja walked home, she suddenly had an idea.
In the evening, she talked to Kerry.
"I don't feel well," she said. "I can't go on the trip tomorrow." 60
She wasn't happy. But she really wanted to see Rhodri during her last day in Wales.

The next morning Kerry went to Carmarthen,
65 and Katja stayed at home. At ten o'clock
she went to the football game. But she didn't
see Rhodri. He wasn't in the team.
"I'm looking for Rhodri. Have you seen him?"
she asked one of the players after the game.
70 "He was late again for training yesterday.
He isn't in the team."

Katja went to Rhodri's house. Maybe he was ill?
"He's gone to Carmarthen," said Rhodri's
mother. "He went out at eight o'clock.
75 He didn't eat breakfast. It'll be very late when he
comes back. And he forgot his mobile phone."

A week later Katja was in Germany.
She got a postcard from Wales. It said:

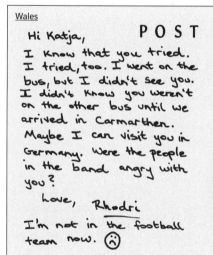

Wales

POST

Hi Katja,
I know that you tried.
I tried, too. I went on the
bus, but I didn't see you.
I didn't know you weren't
on the other bus until we
arrived in Carmarthen.
Maybe I can visit you in
Germany. Were the people
in the band angry with
you?
love, Rhodri
I'm not in the football
team now. ☹

Germany

GREETINGS FROM WALES
COFION O GYMRU

1 Rhodri and Katja

Five of these sentences are right. Find them.

1. Katja wanted to go to the game.
2. The concert was important.
3. Rhodri didn't go to football training.
4. He went to Carmarthen with Katja.
5. Katja went to the game.
6. Katja was on a different bus.
7. Rhodri sent a postcard to Germany.
8. Katja saw Rhodri at the game.
9. Rhodri wants to see Katja again.

2 Partner towns

Is your town twinned with a town in another country? Try to find out:

– What's the name of the town?
– Where is it?
– What's special about the town?
– …

1 A day in Abergavenny

a) Katja wanted to look at Abergavenny. This is what she did.

walk to the market –
interesting

look for a present –
buy a cup

go to the museum –
closed

visit the castle –
look at the dungeon

walk along the river –
see some boats

meet Kerry's friends –
nice

In the evening Katja told Mrs Baker about the day. *Make sentences.*

1. I walked to the market. It was interesting.
2. Then I looked for … . I bought … .
3. After that I … .   *Go on, please.*

b) When Kerry's father came home he had lots of questions about the day in Abergavenny. *Make a dialogue with a partner.*

1. *Mr Baker:* Where did you go today?
   Katja: I … to the market.

2. *Mr Baker:* Did you …?
   Katja: Yes, I did.   *Go on, please.*

… go today?   … meet anybody?

… enjoy it?   … visit any nice places?

… buy anything?   … eat anything?

2 Listening: A trip to Big Pit ◎

Big Pit was a coal mine for 1000 [1] years.

Rabbits [2] worked here every day. It's now a museum.

The tour of the mine is three days [3] long.

You will go 900 [4] metres down the mine.

Over 1,000,000 [5] people visit Big Pit every year.

The museum is open from 05:00 – 24:00 [6].

Listen carefully. Find the right words.

Number 1 is '100'.
Number 2 is … .   *Go on, please.*

3 **An angry coach**

Rhodri's coach was angry after the game. *What's right?*

"Where was Luke?" he shouted loud/loudly . "You were very bad/badly . Mark had the ball, and you didn't see him."
"I'm sorry," said Luke quiet/quietly .
The coach looked angry/angrily at his team. "David, you ran too slow/slowly . We should win these games easy/easily. The other team wasn't good/well . Now go to the changing rooms quick/quickly . I don't want to see you again today. We'll talk about it tomorrow."

Say it!

| That was **loud**. | *Das war **laut**.* |
| He shouted **loudly**. | *Er schrie **laut**.* |

 4 Speaking: **How was it?**

Act dialogues with a partner. Add your own ideas.

A: I went to a party last night.
B: How was it?
A: It was OK.
B: Did you meet anybody?
A: Yes, I met … ./No, … .

Where?	**When?**	**How was it?**
a party	last night	It was OK.
a concert	yesterday	It was cool.
a football game	on Friday	It was awesome.
the leisure centre	at the weekend	It wasn't very good.
…	…	…

5 **Mediation: At the Abergavenny football club**

Some people in the German group are at the Abergavenny football club. They want to know about the club. One of the Germans doesn't speak English, so Katja must help with the information.

> Gegen wen spielt Abergavenny als Nächstes?

> Können wir das Spiel hier in Abergavenny anschauen?

> Wann ist das nächste Heimspiel? Gegen wen spielt Abergavenny?

> Um wie viel Uhr fängt das Spiel an?

Position	Team	Played	Points
1	Monmouth Town	15	39
2	Rogestone	15	39
3	A. C. Pontymiste	16	31
4	Abergavenny	16	27
5	Newtown	13	26

Next away game against	**Next home game** against
Monmouth Town Sat 1st January 2 o'clock	Tillery United Sat 8th January 2 o'clock

TIPP

Arbeiten mit dem Wörterbuch II

Wenn du beim Wörterlernen einmal nicht weißt, wie ein Wort ausgesprochen wird, kannst du in deinem Wörterbuch oder in der alphabetischen Wortliste ab S. 107 ganz einfach die so genannte Lautschrift nachschlagen. Die Lautschrift ist für alle Sprachen gleich und sagt dir genau, wie etwas ausgesprochen wird. Keine Angst, du musst nicht alle Lautschriftzeichen auswendig lernen! Viele sind wie in unserer normalen Schrift. Die anderen Zeichen kannst du jederzeit nachschlagen (S. 91).

Den Umgang mit der Lautschrift kannst du üben. Versuche immer wieder, die Lautschrift im Wörterbuch zu lesen oder auch einmal einzelne Wörter beim Lernen selbst in Lautschrift zu schreiben. Außerdem kannst du die Lautschrift als Geheimsprache verwenden. Kannst du zum Beispiel diesen Text lesen?

he'ləʊ krɪs
haʊ ɑ: ju: kæn wi: mi:t æt sɪks ə'klɒk ɪn frʌnt əv ðə 'swɪmɪŋ pu:l
aɪ wɒnt tʊ tel ju: ə 'si:krət
'li:sə

Lösung: Hello Chris! How are you? Can we meet at six o'clock in front of the swimming pool? I want to tell you a secret. Lisa

6 Word web: Sport and music

Make a word web for 'sport and music' in your exercise book.

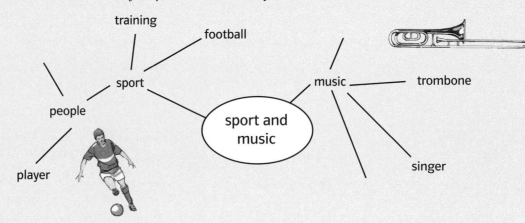

7 Listen and speak 🔘

[w]

What's the **w**eather like in **W**ales?
Very **w**et, they say.
And it's **w**orse in **w**inter.
Well, **w**e'll take **w**arm anoraks.
And **w**e'll eat hot snacks.

8 Mirror words

Can you read these words?
Use a mirror.

watch	morning	language
forget	tonight	postcard

mirror – Spiegel

9 A cartoon

Some Welsh words are very, very long!

"Two 'N's in 'twinned', Gareth!"

▷ 10 Today and yesterday

1

| Let's talk about football. | But we … about that yesterday! |

2

| Look at this magazine. | It's boring. I … at it yesterday. |

3

| Do you want to watch my DVD? | No, thanks. I … it … . |

4

| Don't forget your training today. | I know. I … it … . |

5

| Can you hear that noise? | Yes, I can. I … it …, too. |

6

| Don't sit there! | Why not? I … . |

Write the answers.

1. But we talked about that yesterday!   2. *Go on, please.*

11 What's my job?

1

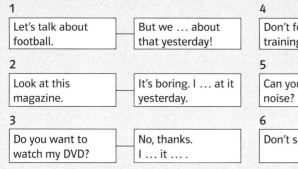

I'm often on the radio.

4

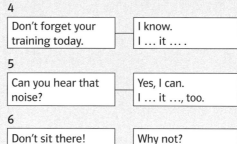

I work in a school. I often repair things.

2

I work in a school. Maths is my subject.

5

I work with football teams.

3

I work in a coal mine.

6

I help people when they're ill.

1. Number 1 is a DJ.   2. Number 2 is … .   *Go on, please.*

Past simple *(Vergangenheit)*

Verwendung:
Du verwendest das past simple, *um über Dinge zu sprechen, die in der Vergangenheit passiert sind.*

I **went** to a concert last night.
I **met** a German girl there.
She **played** in a band.

Bildung:
Meist wird -ed *an das Verb angehängt.*
Es gibt auch unregelmäßige Formen.
Die Formen von be *sind* was *und* were.

He **looked** into his wallet.
Then he **bought** the new computer game.
Where **were** you? – I **was** at home.

Achtung!
Verneinung und Fragen werden mit did
und der Grundform des Verbs gebildet.
Es wird kein -ed *mehr an das Verb angehängt!*

I **didn't see** her yesterday.
Did she **stay** at home?

Welche Beispielsätze passen zu Cartoon A? Warum?

Adjectives and adverbs *(Adjektive und Adverbien)*

Verwendung:
Adjektive beschreiben Personen, Ereignisse und Sachen.
Adverbien beschreiben, wie etwas geschieht.

The job is very **dangerous**.

But he always works **carefully**.

Bildung:
• *Die meisten Adjektive werden durch Anhängen von* -ly *zu Adverbien.*
• *Es gibt aber auch unregelmäßige Formen.*

The trombone is a **nice** instrument.
But only if you play it **nicely**!
It was a very **good** game.
You played **well**.

Achtung!
Im Deutschen gibt es diese Unterscheidung nicht!

Das Spiel war **gut**.
Ihr habt **gut** gespielt.

Welche Beispielsätze passen zu Cartoon B? Warum?

Checklist

Ich kann
... *über Wales sprechen.*
... *fragen, wo jemand war.*
... *sagen, was ich gestern gemacht habe.*
... *sagen, wie etwas war.*
... *fragen, ob jemand etwas vergessen hat.*
... *beschreiben, wie etwas ist.*
... *beschreiben, wie etwas geschieht.*
... *sagen, dass jemand etwas gut kann.*

They speak Welsh in Wales.
Where were you?
I went to a football game.

The concert was great!
Did you forget the training?

This picture is very nice.
She laughed happily.
He sings very well.

Checkout: Two tricks

The hole in the hand
Take a sheet of paper and roll it up. Hold the rolled up sheet of paper close to your left eye.
Look with both your eyes at something about five metres away. Then put your other hand in front of your right eye. There's now a hole in your hand.

The third finger
Put the tips of your index fingers together at eye level in front of your face. Focus on a white wall two or three metres behind your fingers. Pull them apart slowly. You can now see another finger in the middle.

Haben die beiden Tricks bei dir funktioniert?
Hier gibt es wie immer einige Wörter und Wendungen, die du nicht kennst. Du kannst sie aus dem Zusammenhang erschließen oder in der alphabetischen Wortliste ab Seite 107 nachschlagen.

TIPP

Tipps: Two tricks
1. rolled up sheet of paper, hole, index finger: *Diese Dinge siehst du alle in der Zeichnung.*
2. *Habe Geduld und lies den Text mehrere Male durch. Nicht bei jedem funktionieren optische Täuschungen gleich.*

Is school cool?

a You already know lots of things about British schools.
Work in groups and find words for:
school subjects: Maths, …
school people: caretaker, …
school rooms: cafeteria, …

> My name is Alexandra Young.
> I go to Westlands High School. There are over a thousand pupils at my school. We all wear the Westlands uniform, but I don't like it. I hate black shoes.

My school day starts at eight thirty. First we have morning registration. The teacher checks that we are all there. Then we have our lessons. The lunch break is at 12.30. I always eat in the school cafeteria. My favourite meal is fish and chips.

> Alexandra?

> Here!

Grades in Britain:	Grades in Germany:
A	1
B	2
C	3
D	4
E	5/6

We have homework every day. I usually do it in the evening. There are lots of tests, too. I got a B in my last English test. I was happy with that grade.

1 Alexandra's school

What's wrong?

1. Westlands School has got 800 pupils. That's wrong. It's got … .
2. The school day starts at nine o'clock.
3. She never eats in the school cafeteria.
4. Alexandra does her homework in the evening.
5. She got an A in her English test.
6. She hasn't enjoyed History this year.
7. Her project was awful.
8. The art club meets in the lunch break.

2 Two schools

Make notes about the two schools.

Westlands	**My school**
a uniform	no uniform
…	…

> uniform   cafeteria
> day starts at …   reports
> number of pupils   grades   …

Westlands High School

Subject profile: History

Name: *Alexandra Young*
Tutor group: *9GP*
Teacher: *Mr Barnes*

PUPIL

Last year I wasn't really interested in History. This year I've really enjoyed the subject. It's interesting with Mr Barnes. I've tried to work harder this year. I think my work is quite good.

TEACHER

Alexandra has worked hard this term. She has got some good ideas, and she is very interested in History. She always does her homework. Her project about Britain in 1950 was very good.

This is my profile for History. Every year we get a profile for all our subjects. We must write a report and say how good or bad we think we are. Then the teachers write how good or bad we really are.

I'm in the art club. We draw pictures and make things. The club meets every Wednesday after school. My best friend is in the club, too. It's fun!

Sports hall

---

3 Speaking: **A visit**

An English pupil is visiting your school. *Act the dialogue with a partner.*

A: How big is your school?
B: It's got … pupils, I think.
A: When does the school day start?
B: It starts at … .   *Go on, please.*

> Where do you …?   Are there lots of …?
> Do you have …?   …

▷ **4** **A profile**

a) *Write a profile for one of your subjects. Say how good or bad you are.*

b) *Read your friend's profile. Is it true?*

> I'm quite good at … now.
> I think … better this year.
> I've worked … .
> …

b

> A girl in my class never did her homework. First she got detentions. Then her parents had to come to school. It was so embarrassing!

School information

School rules
- You must stay at school during the school day.
- Do not eat and drink in classrooms.
- Always wear a school uniform when you are at school. Pupils may not wear earrings at school.
- Do not use mobile phones during lessons.
- Do not bully other pupils.

Bullying
When pupils bully other pupils, they:
- push or kick them every day.
- say awful things to them every day.
- send them lots of awful text messages.

Westlands School says **NO** to bullying!

School sanctions
Here are some of the school's sanctions:
- Detention (pupils must come after school or on Saturday)
- Letter or phone call to parents
- Pupils must leave the school.
- Parents must come to school and talk to the headteacher.
- Pupils must stay at home for one day.
- Extra homework

5   Rules and sanctions

a) *What must pupils do? What mustn't they do?*
   Make two lists.

must	mustn't
stay at school	eat and drink in classrooms
…	…

b) *Talk about the sanctions with a partner.*

    A: A detention on Saturday is terrible.
    B: I'm not sure. I think it's worse when your parents … .   *Go on, please.*

▷ c) *What rules and sanctions are there at your school? Make two lists.*
   Is your school stricter than Westlands School?

6 Listening with DJ Dan: Four pupils

Today Dan is talking about school rules and
what happens when you break them.
He's talking to four young people.
Two of these sanctions are not in the text.
Which are they?

1. You must give money to the school.
2. A pupil must leave the school.
3. You must go to school with your parents.
4. You get a detention in the lunch break.
5. You get a Saturday detention.
6. You must do extra homework.

7 Writing: What happened?

Write about a situation when you or a friend broke a school rule.
Say what happened.

> I / My friend ran / wore / talked / ... .
> I / He / She ... .
> Then ... .
> …

> The teacher saw / heard / ... .
> He / She gave ... .
> I / We had to ... .
> My / Our parents ... .

8 On the wall

Which is the best message?

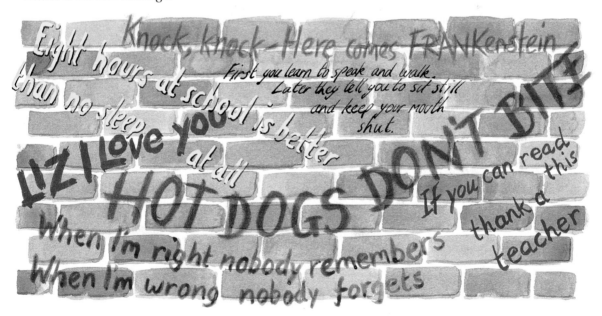

---

knock – *klopfen*; no sleep at all – *überhaupt kein Schlaf*; keep your mouth shut – *den Mund halten*; bite – *beißen*; if – *wenn*

Project: Bullying

Bullying is a problem in lots of schools.

One girl's story
Some pupils are bullying me at school. I tried to talk to them, but it hasn't stopped. They make jokes about the style of my hair. They say I'm a freak. I don't think it will get better.
                    Naomi, 14

Is somebody bullying you?
We can help you!

Childline
0800 11 11
www.childline.org.uk

Work in groups and do a project about bullying. You can show your work to the class in ONE of two different ways.

a short play in English   a poster with rules for your class

Say **NO**
to bullying!

These are our rules
for Class 7d:

Organize your work:

1. Plan it!
   Decide: a play or a poster? Who does which job? Where do you start?

2. Do it!
   Find information and write the texts.
   Play: Think about what you need for the play. Practise the dialogues.
   Poster: Think about a design for your poster and find or draw pictures.

3. Present it!
   Show your poster to the class or act the play for them.

4. Talk about it!
   What was good and what was bad? How can you make it better next time?

Checklist

Ich kann	
...über meine Schule sprechen.	There are over a thousand pupils at my school.
...über meinen Schultag sprechen.	My school day starts at eight thirty.
...über meine Fächer sprechen.	I'm quite good at German.
...über meine Noten sprechen.	I got a B in my last English test.
...über Regeln in der Schule sprechen.	You mustn't use mobile phones at school.
...über Schulstrafen sprechen.	A girl in my class got detentions.
...über Probleme in der Schule sprechen.	Bullying is a problem in our school.

U1 London
U2 Handy
U3 Wales
U4 Schule
U5 Schottland
U6 Musik
U7 Wetter
U8 Sport

Strategy: Writing

Eine kleine Geschichte auf Englisch zu schreiben ist gar nicht so schwer! Hier sind einige Tipps, wie du vorgehen kannst.

A Vor dem Schreiben

- *Du entscheidest dich für ein persönliches Erlebnis, über das du schreiben möchtest, z.B. eine lustige Geschichte aus dem Urlaub, ein Erlebnis in der Schule oder etwas über dein Haustier.*
- *Du schreibst die Fragewörter* who, what, when, where, why, what then *auf ein Blatt Papier. Notiere dir hinter jedem Wort einige Stichpunkte, z. B.*

Who? – my dog Max
What? – ran after the cat

B Während des Schreibens

- *Überlege dir die ersten Sätze, z. B.:*
Last week on Thursday my dog Max ran after our cat. The cat climbed on a tree and Max ... .
- *Schreibe dann die ganze Geschichte auf. Du kannst dich dabei an deinen Notizen zu den Fragewörtern orientieren. Wörter, die du nicht weißt, kannst du auf Deutsch aufschreiben und später im Wörterbuch nachschlagen, z. B.*
They needed a big long *Leiter* to get him out of the tree.

C Nach dem Schreiben

- *Lies die ganze Geschichte durch. Nimm dir Stellen, die sich ,komisch' anhören, noch einmal vor.*
- *Gib die Geschichte einem Partner zum Lesen. Verbessere die Fehler, die er gefunden hat.*
- *Überlege dir eine gute Überschrift für deine Geschichte, z. B: Max's accident.*
- *Gib die Geschichte deiner Lehrerin oder deinem Lehrer zur Korrektur.*
- *Schreibe zum Schluss eine ,saubere' Version deiner Geschichte. Wenn du möchtest, kannst du sie mit Bildern oder Zeichnungen gestalten.*

Grammar

1 Questions and answers

Find the right answers.

1. What would you like to do in London?
2. Have you got any ideas for tomorrow?
3. Can I wear my old T-shirt and jeans?
4. How can I go to the Science Museum?
5. Have you got a new mobile phone?
6. Can I use your mum's computer?
7. Why were you late yesterday?
8. Where can we meet after school?

No, I haven't. My old one is OK.
You can take the Underground.
Let's meet in the new café. It's cool!
I'd like to visit the West End.
No, you ought to wear nice clothes.
I went shopping and forgot to call you.
I could show you the London Eye.
I'm not sure. I'll ask my mum first.

2 Good tips

What's missing?

must (2x)	mustn't (3x)	ought to (3x)

1. This was the last time! You … be late for training again.
2. You … help your friend with his Maths homework. He helped you with German.
3. You … use your mobile phone during lessons.
4. You … stay at school during the school day.
5. He … do more sport, but he's very lazy.
6. You … do this diet every day or it won't help.
7. You … bully other pupils. That's awful!
8. She … write this again, but I don't think there is enough time.

3 Speaking: Did you forget …?

Make dialogues with a partner.

You	Your partner
Frage, ob er/sie euer Treffen gestern vergessen hat.	Sage ja. Entschuldige dich.
Frage, wo er/sie war.	Sage, dass du auf dem Markt warst.
Frage, ob es ihm gefallen hat und ob er etwas gekauft hat.	Sage, dass es sehr cool war. Du hast ein schönes Geschenk für einen Freund/ eine Freundin gekauft.
Sei empört. Sage, dass du ihn/sie nicht mehr sehen möchtest.	Sage, dass es dir Leid tut. Schlage vor, morgen darüber zu reden.
Verabschiede dich.	Verabschiede dich.

Words

4 The wrong word

a) *Find the wrong word.*

1. caretaker – headmaster – teacher – driver – pupils
2. English – Welsh – France – German – Chinese
3. do it – listen to it – talk about it – plan it – present it
4. awful – great – awesome – fantastic – cool
5. concert – sing – message – audition – dance
6. plan – bill – topic – network – ring tone

b) *Make an English-German list of the words.*

> caretaker – Hausmeister
> headmaster –

5 How can you do it?

a) *How can you speak? Make a word web.*

1.

quietly   well

loudly   **speak**

well	badly
quickly	slowly
loudly	quietly
angrily	crazily
happily	…

b) *How can you run, dance, …? Make word webs for these words.*

1. run	5. eat
2. dance	6. sing
3. shout	7. play the guitar
4. draw	8. play football

6 Topics

Write a short text about one of these topics. Tell your class about it.

Wales	**My mobile phone**	**London**
language	cheap	interesting sights
towns	expensive	museums
museums	old	palaces
sports	modern	festivals
how many people	I can …	Underground
…	I use it for …	…

Scotland

What you can do in Scotland

a Scotland has got lots of mountains and large lakes. It's very nice in summer, but it often rains. In winter it can be very cold. Many people come to Scotland to enjoy nature.

There are lots of activities in the mountains. Climb Ben Nevis! It's the highest mountain in Scotland.

Look for Nessie the Monster! People say she lives in Loch Ness. 'Loch' is the Scottish word for a lake.

Not many people live in Scotland.
Germany: about 82 million
England: about 50 million
Scotland: about 5 million

Ride a bike along a bike route or sit on a beach.

Many people visit the city of Edinburgh. They look at the famous castle, or they go to the Edinburgh Festival.

Where you can stay in Scotland

The Ness House B & B

5 bedrooms
£25-£32 per
person per
night

Lots of tourists stay in a 'bed and breakfast'. These are rooms in a small private house.

Oban Hostel

£13.50 per night
in July and
August
Children £11.75

Scotland's youth hostels are often in the most beautiful places. You have to sleep in a room with other people. There's usually a kitchen and a games room, too.

Jenny's Cottage

Two bedrooms, bathroom, living room with TV, kitchen.
£475 per week (July/August)
Sorry, no pets!

Some families like to stay in a cottage. They can cook their own meals.

---

1 The right information

a) *These sentences are wrong. What's the right information?*

1. Lots of people live in Scotland.
2. There are no mountains and lakes.
3. The weather is nice in winter, but it often rains.
4. People think a monster lives on Ben Nevis.
5. There is a famous lake in Edinburgh.
6. Nessie is the name of a lake.

b) *Where would you like to stay?*
Say why.

2 Speaking: A holiday in Scotland?

a) Your partner wants to go to Scotland.
Act the dialogue.

A: When do you want to go to Scotland?
B: In July, maybe for one week .
A: What would you like to do?
B: I'd like to ride along a bike route .
A: Where are you going to stay?
B: In a youth hostel .
A: I hope you have a good time.

b) *Make new dialogues.*

May, 10 days?	climb Ben Nevis
August,	look for Nessie
2 weeks …	…

cottage   youth hostel B & B …

3 Listening: Two holidays ◎

Simon and Gemma are talking about their holidays in Scotland.
Listen and take notes.

1. Did Simon enjoy his holiday?
   Say why or why not.
2. Did Gemma enjoy her holiday?
   Say why or why not.

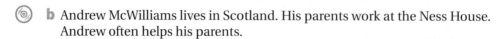

b Andrew McWilliams lives in Scotland. His parents work at the Ness House. Andrew often helps his parents.

Today Andrew is in the kitchen. His parents are making breakfast for their guests. Mr McWilliams has just been in the dining room.

"Mrs Schmidt has just come down," he says. "She's ordered a vegetarian breakfast."

"I've already made one," says Mrs McWilliams. "Can you take it to her, Andrew?"

"Mr and Mrs Uddin have asked for orange juice," says Mr McWilliams. "And their daughter has just broken a cup."

"Andrew, go and tidy up, please. Oh, you haven't taken the toast to Mrs Schmidt yet," says Mrs McWilliams.

"And you haven't carried Mrs Spencer's bags to her car," shouts Mr McWilliams. "You haven't done anything yet."

"Just a minute, please. I can't do everything, Dad," says Andrew. "I'm not Superman."

Say it!

She**'s ordered** a vegetarian breakfast. You **haven't taken** the toast to Mrs Schmidt yet.	Sie **hat** ein vegetarisches Frühstück **bestellt**. Du **hast** Frau Schmidt den Toast noch **nicht gebracht**.

---

4 So much stress!

1. Mr McWilliams has just been in the dining room.
2. Mrs Schmidt … . *Go on, please.*
3. The Uddins … .
4. Their daughter … .
5. Andrew hasn't … .
6. And he hasn't … .

> … a vegetarian breakfast
> … orange juice
> … Mrs Spencer's bags …
> … a cup
> … the dining room …
> … the toast …

---

5 Speaking: I haven't done it yet!

a) *Write two sentences. Write what you've done this week and what you haven't done. Write your name.*

b) *Give your card to your partner. Your partner must tell the class what you've done and what you haven't done.*

> I've finished my Geography project.
> I haven't done my Maths homework yet.
> Max

> I've visited my uncle and my cousins this week. I haven't visited any friends.
> Andrea

Max has finished his Geography project. He hasn't done his Maths homework yet.

c The people in the Ness House often ask Andrew questions.

> Have you booked our boat trip on the lake yet?

> I've lost my dog. Has he been in the garden?

> Yes, I have. He isn't there.

> Have you ever seen Nessie?

> Have you ever been to Germany?

> No, I haven't. I'll do it now.

> No, he hasn't. Have you looked in the car park?

> Maybe he's jumped in the lake. Maybe Nessie has already eaten him.

> No, I haven't. But people have seen strange things on the lake.

> Yes, I have.

RECEPTION

Say it!

Have you **booked** our boat trip yet?   *Hast* du unsere Bootsfahrt schon *gebucht?*

Have you **ever been** to Germany?   *Warst* du *schon einmal* in Deutschland?

6 Has he or hasn't he?

Match the parts of the sentences.

1. Andrew hasn't   been in the garden.
2. The girl has   seen Nessie.
3. The dog hasn't   already eaten the dog.
4. Maybe Nessie has   seen strange things on the lake.
5. Andrew has never   lost her dog.
6. But people have   booked the boat trip yet.

7 Speaking: Have you ever . . . ?

Ask your partner.

1. *A:* Have you ever seen
   a photo of Nessie?
   B: No, I haven't. Not yet!
2. *A:* ... .   Go on, please.

seen a photo of Nessie?
lost/found a pet?
stayed in a hotel?
helped in a shop or hotel?
been to Berlin?
visited a famous castle?

Yes, I have.
No, I haven't.
Not yet!

A photo of Nessie?

One day in August a family arrived at the Ness House for their summer holiday.
They had a son, Tom, and a daughter, Helen. Tom was 13, like Andrew.
"Your son can play football with our son, Andrew," said Mr McWilliams.

The next day Tom met Andrew and they
5 played football in the garden. Later they
sat down and talked.
"Does Nessie really live in Loch Ness?"
asked Tom. "And have you seen her?"
Andrew laughed. "Everybody asks me
10 this," he said. "I don't go to the lake
very often. I have sometimes seen
something in the lake. But when it's
dark, you can't be sure."
"Where's the best place to look?"
15 Tom asked.

"I know a good place," said Andrew.
"Some people have seen something
there. You should go before it's dark.
You can go there this evening. But I
can't come with you. I want to visit a   20
friend."
"OK. But why should I go so late?"
"I think Nessie comes up to breathe
before it gets dark," answered Andrew.
Tom laughed.   25
"Let's go," said Andrew. "I'll show you
where the place is."

Andrew and Tom walked out of the
garden. They took a path to the lake.
Andrew found a place near some   30
bushes.
"This is the place," said Andrew.
"I'm not sure you'll see anything, but
take a camera. You could be lucky."
"OK, I'll come back later with   35
a camera."
The two boys walked back to the house.
"Sorry, I can't come with you," said
Andrew, "but I'll be at my friend's
house."   40

In the evening Tom's sister wanted to come with him. Tom and Helen took the same path before it was dark.
45 They sat down and waited. Tom had his camera. It was very quiet on the lake. They couldn't hear anything. It was almost dark, so they
50 couldn't see much on the water. Tom looked at his watch.

Suddenly they heard a noise. "What was that?" asked Helen. Tom got up and looked over the water.
55 "I don't know," he said after a minute. They could see something on the dark water. "Look," said Helen. "Is that Nessie's head?" Something went slowly through the
60 water and made a strange noise. "Andrew was right." Tom was sure now. "She comes up in the evening to breathe." "Take a photo quickly, maybe we can
65 sell it," said Helen. Tom took the photo. But then he was worried. "I think Nessie has seen us. She's swimming to us."

Tom and Helen ran back along the path to the Ness House. 70

Behind the bushes Andrew and his friend tried not to laugh. Andrew's friend took his model of a boat with Nessie's head out of the water. Andrew put the remote control in a bag. They 75 walked back to his friend's house. When they were in the house, they started to laugh loudly. Andrew and his friend loved these jokes. They were the best thing about Loch Ness. 80

Back in the lake, something swam quietly through the dark water …

---

1 **Three texts**

Two of the texts have got wrong information in them. Which text is right?

1. Tom played football with Andrew. Then the two boys went to the lake. They saw something in the water. Tom took a photo of Nessie, but Helen played a trick on them.

2. Tom and his sister were in the Ness House with their parents. One day they took a photo of Nessie. But Tom knew that Nessie was a model of a boat.

3. One evening Tom and his sister went to Loch Ness. They saw something in the water and Tom took a photo. They were scared. They didn't know it was a trick.

▷ **2** **Andrew's story**

Andrew wants to tell his friends about the trick. *Tell his story.*

This is so funny. A boy and a girl are staying at the Ness House. I played football with … . He asked me about … . I took him … . In the evening my friend and I … .

1 Activities in Scotland

What have these people just done?

1. They've just climbed a mountain.
2. She's … .
   Go on, please.

climb a mountain	visit a museum
see Nessie	take a photo of the castle
ride along a bike route	swim in the sea

2 So busy!

What has Andrew done?
What hasn't he done? Make sentences.

1. Andrew has booked a boat trip
   for Mrs Schmidt.
2. He hasn't … .
   Go on, please.

> **Andrew**
> *book a boat trip for Mrs Schmidt* ✓
> *tidy up the kitchen* ✗
> *check the e-mail* ✓
> *look for the girl's dog* ✗
> *take the new TV to room 7* ✓
> …

3 Listening: Tammy the marathon swimmer ◎

What's the right answer?

1. Tammy is from …
   a) Scotland,
   b) Australia,
   c) England.

2. Tammy swam for …
   a) 6 hours and 9 minutes,
   b) 9 hours and 6 minutes,
   c) 3 hours and 9 minutes.

3. Loch Ness is …
   a) very cold,
   b) not so cold,
   c) like a swimming pool.

4. When Tammy swims, she remembers …
   a) jokes,
   b) music,
   c) Maths problems.

4 Speaking: **Lucy and Sarah**

Lucy is in a youth hostel with her friend Sarah.

Act the dialogue with a partner.

Lucy: We must leave early tomorrow.
Have you checked the bus times yet?
Sarah: Yes, I have. I checked them last night.
Lucy: Have you phoned your parents yet?
Sarah: Yes, I have. I … them at six o'clock.
Go on, please.

Check the bus times?	… last night.
Answer your e-mails?	… this morning.
Buy a present for your mum?	… on Monday.
Phone your parents?	… at six o'clock.
Send a postcard?	… yesterday.
Pack all your clothes?	… an hour ago.

▷ 5 Speaking: **At the information centre**

Jenny works at the information centre.
Some young people would like to visit
different places.
Make dialogues with a partner.

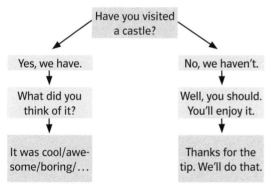

1. visit a castle

2. climb Ben Nevis

3. ride along bike route

4. see the Loch Ness
   Monster Exhibition

6 **Mediation: In a youth hostel**

You're in a youth hostel. A German girl, Gina, has problems with English.
Help her to talk to the man from the youth hostel.

Gina: Ich habe drei Tage gebucht, aber ich würde gerne eine Woche in der
Jugendherberge bleiben.
You: My friend has booked … .
Man: She can only stay five days. After that a group from Italy will come here.
You: …
Gina: Kannst du ihn fragen, ob es andere Jugendherbergen in der Nähe gibt?
You: …
Man: Yes, there's a nice youth hostel near here. I can phone for her.
You: …
Gina: Danke, das ist sehr nett von ihm.
You: …

Arbeiten mit dem Wörterbuch III

Ein Wort, das du nicht kennst, kannst du im Wörterbuch nachschlagen. Aber aufgepasst, ein Wort kann trotzdem ganz verschiedene Bedeutung haben! Nimm zum Beispiel diesen Satz:

It was a very hot day.
But we had a big <u>fan</u> in our room,
so it was nice and cool.

Von was ist hier die Rede? Schlage das Wort *fan* in einem Wörterbuch nach. Du wirst sehen, dass es zwei sehr unterschiedliche Dinge bedeuten kann. Was passt in diesem Zusammenhang?

Hier sind noch einige weitere Beispiele. Die unterstrichenen Wörter kennst du eigentlich schon. Aber passt die bisherige Bedeutung hier? Schlage die Wörter nach und überlege was richtig ist.

1. The best team will win a <u>cup</u>.
2. I looked down into the <u>well</u> but I couldn't see any water.
3. Don't park the car here. You'll get a <u>ticket</u>!

---

7 **Word web: Nature**

Make a word web for 'nature' in your exercise book.

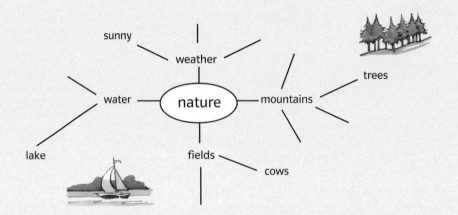

---

8 **Match the words**

1. 'Mountain' goes with 'climb'.
   You can climb a mountain.
2. 'Bike' goes with … .
   Go on, please.

mountain • bike	stay • swim
lake • hotel	climb • drive
meal • air	order • ride
trip • car	breathe • book

▷ **9** **Listen and speak: Same sound, different spelling** 🔊

a) *One word hasn't got a long [u:] sound. Find it.*

1. argue   you   make   pupil
2. museum   town   food   shoe
3. green   fruit   blue   uniform
4. Tuesday   new   knew   leave
5. room   group   knife   spoon

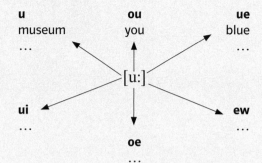

u
museum
...

ou
you

ue
blue
...

[u:]

ui
...

oe
...

ew
...

b) *Put the words in different groups.*

10 **The Edinburgh Festival**

What's missing?

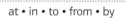

at • in • to • from • by

When is it?
The Edinburgh Festival takes place every year ... summer. People come ... the festival ... many different countries.

What can I do?
You can listen ... music and you can go ... lots of different events. There are more than 100 different events.

How can I get there and where can I stay?
You can go ... Edinburgh ... train or you can take a flight there. Many people stay ... hotels. But you can also go ... a bed and breakfast. Other people stay ... a campsite. They go ... bus ... the events. You can buy some tickets ... the tourist information centre.

11 **Do you know?**

What do people in Scotland call six rainy weeks?

summer.

Present perfect *(Perfekt)*

Verwendung:
Du verwendest das present perfect,

- *um zu sagen, was gerade eben*
  passiert ist,

- *um zu sagen, was bereits erledigt ist,*

- *um darüber zu sprechen, was du*
  schon einmal erlebt oder getan hast.

Bildung:
Das present perfect *wird mit einer Form*
von have *und der dritten Verbform*
gebildet.

Achtung!
Hier gibt es viele unregelmäßige Formen
(siehe Tabelle S. 132)!

Achtung Zeitvergleich!
Das present perfect *wird verwendet, um*
auszudrücken, ob man etwas überhaupt
getan hat.

Das past simple *wird verwendet, um*
zu sagen, dass man etwas zu einem
bestimmten Zeitpunkt getan und
abgeschlossen hat.

She **has** just **broken** a cup.
They**'ve ordered** an English breakfast.

I**'ve** already **made** their breakfast.
But I **haven't tidied up** their room yet.

Have you ever **seen** Nessie?
No, I **haven't**. But I**'ve seen** a ghost!

I **have washed** my trousers.
She **has taken** lots of photos.

take – took – **taken**
see – saw – **seen**
read – read – **read** *(Aussprache!)*

Have you **done** your homework?
Yes, I **have**. Here it is!

When **did** you **do** your homework?
I **did** it yesterday evening.

Welche Beispielsätze passen zu den beiden Cartoons? Warum?

Checklist

Ich kann

… sagen, was ich schon erledigt habe.	I've washed it already.
… sagen, was ich noch nicht erledigt habe.	I haven't tidied up my room yet.
… fragen, ob jemand etwas schon erledigt hat.	Have you done your homework yet?
… fragen, ob jemand etwas schon einmal gemacht hat.	Have you ever played cricket?
… fragen, wo jemand schon einmal gewesen ist.	Have you ever been to Scotland?
… sagen, dass ich etwas noch nie getan habe.	I've never stayed in a hotel.
… jemandem Fragen zu seinem Urlaub stellen.	When do you want to go to Scotland?

Checkout: A bad idea!

A boy called Fred Wilder entered a doughnut shop in a small village in Arkansas. He put a pillowcase over his head and shouted at the man behind the counter to give him all the money. Then Wilder realized that something wasn't right – he had forgotten to cut eyeholes in his pillowcase!
So he raised it a bit to see what he was doing. One of the other people in the shop recognized Wilder when he did this and later told the police his name. The police soon found him and sent him to prison. His story was in all the newspapers and the whole nation laughed at him – what a dummy!

Schlechte Idee, schlechte Ausführung. Am besten lässt man ganz die Finger von „krummen Dingern“.
Hast du verstanden, warum alle über Fred Wilder lachen?
Hier gibt es wieder einige Wörter und Wendungen, die du nicht kennst. Du kannst sie aus dem Zusammenhang erschließen oder in der alphabetischen Wortliste ab Seite 107 nachschlagen.

TIPP

Tipps: A bad idea!
1. had forgotten: *Diese Vergangenheitsform von* forget *ist so ähnlich wie im Deutschen.*
2. was doing: *Das ist die Vergangenheitsform von* is doing.
3. pillowcase, counter, doughnut: *Diese Dinge sind alle auf dem Bild zu sehen.*

My music

a

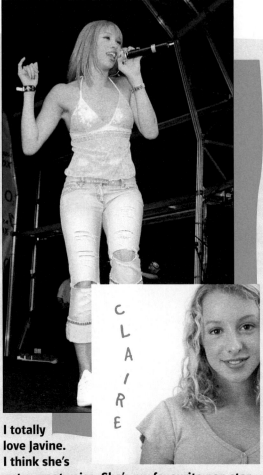

ALEX

CLAIRE

I sing in a heavy metal band with my friends. We practise every week. Music is very important for me, but I don't like jazz or classical music. I've got a CD player and a radio in my room. I also download music from the internet, and I've got an MP3 player that can play 20,000 songs.

I totally love Javine. I think she's got a great voice. She's my favourite pop star. I listen to 'Missing you' every day. I always play it loudly. I've just broken up with my boyfriend, so it really helps. You can't see my bedroom walls. I've got so many posters of her. She's the best!

1   Who's who?

1. ... played an instrument but didn't enjoy the lessons.
   – That's Justin.
2. ... has got lots of posters of a singer.
   – That's ... . *Go on, please.*
3. ... is a singer in a band. Music is very important for him/her.
4. ... listens to the same song every day.
5. ... downloads music.
6. ... sometimes listens to the radio, but isn't so interested in music.

2   Music words

Make groups with the words on these pages. You can add your own words.

Music styles: heavy metal, ...
Instruments: recorder, ...
Groups: band, ...
How you can listen to music: radio, ...

JUSTIN

I had recorder lessons at my old school. The teacher was very strict, and her lessons were so boring. My cousin plays the trumpet in her school orchestra. That's a much better instrument. I sometimes listen to music on the radio, but I'm not so interested in it.

A questionnaire about music

1. Who's your favourite band or singer?
2. Why do you like him/her/them?
3. What's your favourite song?
4. Is there a song that reminds you of a person or special event?
5. Do you and your friends like the same music?
6. When do you listen to music?
7. Are your parents angry when you play music loudly?
8. Do you listen to the radio?
9. Do you buy CDs or do you download music from the internet?
10. Do you play an instrument? (What?)
11. No? Would you like to play an instrument?
12. What instrument would you like to play?
13. Can you read music?

Say it!

Music is very important for me.
Musik ist sehr wichtig für mich.
I totally love Javine.
Ich mag Javine sehr.

3 Speaking: Your music

a) *Work with a partner. One of you asks the questions from the questionnaire. The other answers them.*

A: Who's your favourite band or singer?
B: I totally love ... .
A: Why do you like them/him/her?
B: He's got a great voice.
A: *Go on, please.*

b) *Tell the class about six of your partner's answers.*

Christof's favourite band is ... .
His favourite song is ... .
He often listens to music ... .
Go on, please.

b Tell us what you think about your favourite singer or band! Why do you like them? Are you angry or unhappy with them? Then write to us. The best letters and e-mails will win a cool prize.

You can also text us.

McFly: Why can't all boys be so good-looking?

I totally love McFly. They're so cool. Why aren't the boys in my school so good-looking?
   Kelly, Cardiff

I couldn't believe it when Matrix split. I'm so upset. My friends and I wore black for one week.
   Jade, London

I like Katie Young's music. I really like the lyrics. She sings about problems that I have. She really understands me and my problems.
   Emma, Birmingham

Yellow are an awesome band. They're the best. I like the clothes that they wear.
   Ben, London

I was shocked to see a photo of Mark from Yellow with his girlfriend. In every interview he always says he doesn't have a girlfriend. Pop stars have to say things like that, so that they'll be more popular with girls and sell more CDs. That makes me really angry!
   Tara, London

I really hate Katie Young. I think her last CD was awful. I don't have one friend that has bought it. I don't know why people listen to her.
   Luke, Bristol

Say it!
I like the clothes **that** they wear.
*Ich mag die Kleidung, **die** sie tragen.*

4 Titles and texts

Match these titles with the texts.

1. I think 'Really good-looking boys' is the title for Kelly's text.
2. *Go on, please.*

Her problems are my problems. · We're so upset! · Great clothes, great music.

She's awful. · Tell us what's true! · Really good-looking boys

5 Speaking: **Do you know . . . ?**

Work with a partner. Ask questions.

A: Do you know a British band that is
   very popular in Germany?
B: Yes, I do. I think … are popular now.
   Do you know a German singer
   that …?
A: Yes, I do.   *Go on, please.*

> a British band/is popular in Germany?
> a German singer/is very popular?
> the song/is number 1 this week?
> a group/split this year?
> the names of the boys/sing in …?
> a DJ/plays good music?
> … / …

6 Listening with DJ Dan: Young people and music

Dan is talking to some young people about music.
Listen and take notes.
What problems have Mark, Lisa and Scott got?

name	problem
Mark	…
Lisa	…
…	…

7 Writing: A letter to a magazine

Write to a magazine.
You can write …   *or you can write …*

… a fan letter about a band or a singer.   … a letter that says why you don't like a
Why are they so great?   group or a singer. Why are they so awful?

8 A song: She left me   Fletcher, Thomas Michael/Bourne, James Elliot

Listen to this song. It's by McFly.

She walked in and said   Since she left me,
She didn't wanna know anymore.   She told me
Before I could ask why   Don't worry,
She was gone out the door.   You'll be OK, you don't need me.
I didn't know, what I did wrong,   Believe me you'll be fine!
But now I just can't move on.   Then I knew what she meant,
                                       And it's not what she said,
                                       Now I can't believe that she's gone.

> she didn't wanna know anymore – *sie wollte nichts mehr hören*; just – *einfach*; move on –
> *weitermachen*; since – *seit*; Don't worry – *Mach' dir keine Sorgen*; what she meant – *was sie*
> *meinte*

Project: Profile of a band

*Make a profile of a band. You can
work alone or in small groups.
The band can be:*
    a famous one like the Beatles
    your favourite band
    a band in your town
    an orchestra
    …

Your profile can look like this:

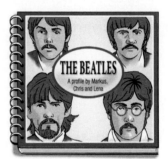

1. *Decide which band you would like to
write about. Find information about
the band and pictures.*

2. *Here are some ideas for the pages of your profile. Use the information and the
pictures that you found. The profile should also have a cover.*

> **Style of music and songs**
> What is the band's style of music? What are the band's best or most famous
> songs?
>
> **People in the band**
> Who plays which instrument? Who is / are the singer(s)? Find information
> about the people in the band and pictures of them.
>
> **History of the band**
> When did the band start? Did the band have a different name? Has anybody
> left the band? Can you find older pictures of the band?
>
> **CDs**
> What are the titles of the band's CDs? When did they make the CDs? (You can
> also give the CDs grades, 'A' for very good and 'E' for awful.)
>
> **Websites**
> Make a list of some of the websites about the band. Write a short text about
> the best or worst websites. Have they got interesting information? Do the links
> work?

3. *When you have all finished your profiles you can have a book party in the
classroom. (Maybe you can send an invitation to your Music teacher!) Tell the
other groups what you think is good/not so good about their profiles.*

Checklist

Ich kann	
… sagen, dass ich selbst Musik mache.	I play an instrument.
… sagen, wie oft ich übe.	I practise every week.
… sagen, welche Musik ich gut finde.	I totally love Javine. She's my favourite singer.
… sagen, wie ich Musik höre.	I've got an MP3 player that can play 20,000 songs.
… jemanden nach seinen musikalischen Interessen fragen.	Who's your favourite singer?
… sagen, warum ich eine Band gut finde.	I really like their lyrics. They understand my problems.
… fragen, ob eine Band bekannt ist.	Are they popular?

Strategy: Speaking

Freies Sprechen in einer Fremdsprache ist oft schwieriger als Lesen und Schreiben. Hier gibt es ein paar Tipps und Tricks, die dir dabei helfen können:

Wenn du vor der Klasse sprichst:

- *Benutze kurze, einfache Sätze. Packe nicht zu viel in jeden Satz hinein. Drei kurze Sätze sind besser als ein langer Satz.*

I like heavy metal.
I often go to concerts.
Last week I heard a very good band.

- *Während der Vorbereitung musst du deinen Text so oft wie möglich laut üben. Am besten übst du vor dem Spiegel.*

Wenn du mit anderen sprichst:

- *Wenn du jemanden nicht verstanden hast, kannst du um Hilfe oder Wiederholung bitten.*

Excuse me?

What does this word mean?

Can you say that again, please?

Can you speak more slowly?

- *Überlege, bevor du sprichst. Wenn du mehr Zeit brauchst, kannst du die folgenden Lückenfüller verwenden.*

Well …

That's a very good question.

Just a minute, please.

Hm ….

Let me think for a minute.

Crazy weather

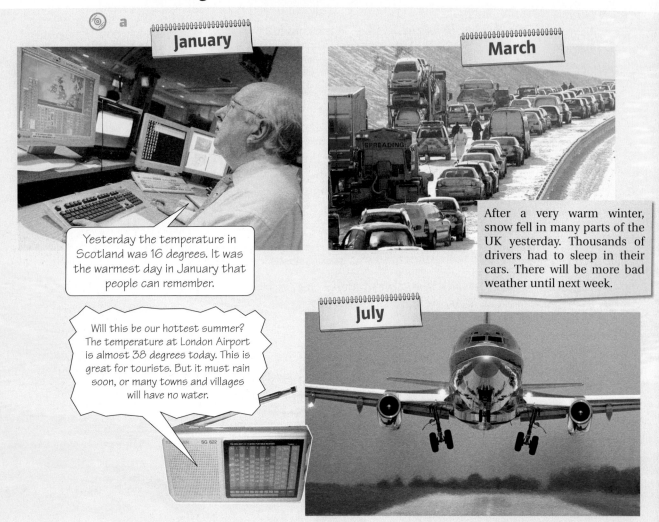

January

Yesterday the temperature in Scotland was 16 degrees. It was the warmest day in January that people can remember.

March

After a very warm winter, snow fell in many parts of the UK yesterday. Thousands of drivers had to sleep in their cars. There will be more bad weather until next week.

Will this be our hottest summer? The temperature at London Airport is almost 38 degrees today. This is great for tourists. But it must rain soon, or many towns and villages will have no water.

July

---

1 Headlines!

Match the headlines with the stories.

> A summer like no other
> Thousands of drivers can't leave their cars
> A tornado comes to the south coast
> Floods in many parts of the country
> Warmest day in winter

1. The first headline goes with July.
2. The second headline … .
   Go on, please.

2 Through the year

Make sentences.

1. Jan./temperature/Scotland/
   16 degrees
   In January the temperature in
   Scotland was 16 degrees.
2. Mar./snow/many parts/UK
   Go on, please.
3. Jul./temperature/London
   Airport/almost 38 degrees
4. Oct./shops and houses/under
   water
5. Nov./tornado/south coast/
   England

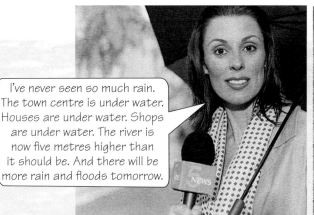

October

I've never seen so much rain. The town centre is under water. Houses are under water. Shops are under water. The river is now five metres higher than it should be. And there will be more rain and floods tomorrow.

November

NEWS

Weather

Last night a tornado came to the south coast of England. The wind destroyed houses, trees and a campsite. There has never been a storm like this in the UK.
Click here for more stories.

Internet

Say it!

There **will be** more bad weather until next week.
The temperature **is** 38 degrees today.

Das Wetter **bleibt** bis nächste Woche schlecht.
Heute **haben wir** 38 Grad.

3 Listening: The weather report 🎧

What will the weather be like in England, in Scotland and in Wales?
Listen and take notes.

England	Scotland	Wales
…	…	…

4 Speaking: Crazy weather?

What crazy weather can you remember?
Make notes. Then tell the class about your crazy weather.

the warmest/coldest/… that I can …
the temperature was …
never seen so much …
… was under water
… had to …
…

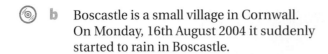

b Boscastle is a small village in Cornwall. On Monday, 16th August 2004 it suddenly started to rain in Boscastle.

> Boscastle is in a valley near the sea. Many tourists visit the popular Museum of Witchcraft in the village.

> If it rains again tomorrow, we won't stay in Boscastle.

> If it rains, we'll need our anoraks. They're in the car.

> If we go to that café, we can wait until it stops.

> If the weather is better tomorrow, we'll go to the beach.

Say it!

If it **rains**, we**'ll need** our anoraks.
If it **rains** tomorrow, we **won't stay** here.

*Wenn es **regnet**, **brauchen** wir unsere Anoraks.*
*Wenn es morgen **regnet**, **bleiben** wir **nicht** hier.*

5 That's wrong!

1. Boscastle is in a valley near a lake.
   That's wrong! It's in a valley near the sea.
2. It hasn't got a museum.
   Go on, please.
3. If it's sunny, the tourists will need their anoraks.
4. The anoraks are at the beach.
5. If the weather is better tomorrow, they'll go to a café.
6. If it rains again, they'll go to the Museum of Witchcraft.
7. If they go to the café, they can find out about witchcraft.

6 Speaking: Weekend plans

a) What will you do at the weekend?
   Make two lists.

b) *Make dialogues with a partner.*

go on a
camping trip
play football
…

stay at home
go to the leisure
centre
…

A: What will you do at the weekend?
B: If the weather is nice, I'll go on a camping trip.
A: And if it rains?
B: If it rains, I won't go on a camping trip. I'll … then.

c Andrew Williams is a pilot. On 16th August his helicopter flew to Boscastle.

"We left at four o'clock. I flew the helicopter myself. The storm was very bad. We saw that the village was under water. People were on their houses and in trees. Some stood on cars, but the water carried the cars into the sea. It was a disaster."

The pilots saved about 60 people. They pulled people out of houses and out of trees. Many people tried to save themselves. One girl pulled herself from the river.

Kate:

I was in Boscastle with my parents. I saw the disaster myself. The water destroyed cars, houses, shops. There were pets in some of the cars. It's a pity that we couldn't save them. You feel angry with yourself because you can't help them.

Say it!

Many people tried to save **themselves**.
> *Viele Menschen versuchten,*
> *sich zu retten.*

I saw the disaster **myself**.
> *Ich habe die Katastrophe*
> *selbst gesehen.*

7 A disaster

A reporter has made some notes about the disaster.
Write what happened.

On August 16th there was a very bad storm in … . *Go on, please.*

> *August 16th – a very bad storm*
> *so much rain – village under water*
> *people on houses / in trees / on cars –*
> *4 o'clock – helicopters – flew to village –*
> *pulled people from trees – couldn't save*
> *pets – …*

8 Speaking: Do you do it yourself?

a) *Make two lists.*

do it myself	don't do it myself
…	…

> do my homework   make my bed
> tidy up …   repair …
> buy …   cook …
> …

b) *Talk about your lists with a partner.*

A: I always do my homework myself. And you?
B: I usually do it myself. But my brother sometimes helps me with Maths.
I always make my bed myself. Do you do that yourself, too?
A: Go on, please.

Before you read:
Look at page 67 again. Who is Kate Benson and why was she in Boscastle?
Then look at the pictures here. What did Kate do when the water came?

The storm

Kate Benson, her older sister Susie and their parents were in Boscastle. It was
August, and it was a rainy afternoon. They left their car in the car park and walked
into the village. All the tourists wore anoraks as they walked in and out of the
shops and cafés. Some went down the road to the sea. Others came slowly back.

"What would you like to do?" asked   5
Kate's mother.
"It's so boring," said Susie.
"It's still raining," said Kate's father.
"Should we drive back to the cottage?"
"We can wait here until it stops," said   10
Kate's mother.
Suddenly Susie said, "Let's go to the
Museum of Witchcraft. That'll be cool."
"OK," said Kate's mother. "You two can
go in there and we'll look at the shops."   15

Kate and Susie went into the museum.
They looked at the exhibition.
The museum was dark. Outside they
could hear the storm and the rain.
"Listen to the storm," said Susie.   20
"The witches are coming. Look."
Kate saw a model of a witch in black
clothes and with a black hat.

"She'll come through your bedroom
window in the night," said Susie.   25
"Stop it," said Kate.
Suddenly, a window broke.
Kate was so scared, she screamed.
Then a door broke. People started
to shout and scream as water came   30
into the museum. It came through
the door and windows.
"What's happening?" screamed Kate.
"I don't know," said Susie.

35 There was lots of water in the museum now. Parts of the exhibition fell into the
water. Outside there was a large river between the houses and shops. It carried
cars, trees, tables, boxes through the village to the sea. People tried to climb away
from the water.
Kate suddenly screamed. A dead woman was in the water. Kate saw her black hair
40 and the black clothes.
"It isn't a woman," shouted Susie. "It's the model of the witch from the museum."

The water in the museum was now very high. Kate and Susie climbed the stairs. As they climbed, the water followed
45 them. Suddenly they heard a loud noise outside. They ran into a room and opened a window. They saw helicopters over the village. A helicopter flew over the museum where Kate and Susie
50 were. A line came down from the helicopter. A man in a uniform came down with the line.
"Come quickly," said the man.
The man took Kate and the pilot pulled
55 her up to the helicopter.
In the helicopter she saw her parents. They were cold and wet.
Then the man went down again and saved her sister.
60 "You were very lucky," said the man in the uniform. "Your parents saw you."
As they all looked out of the helicopter, a shop near the museum fell into the water.

65 Later in the evening Kate and Susie were with their parents in their holiday cottage and saw pictures of Boscastle on TV.
"This is just like a disaster film," said Kate's father. "But it happened and we were all in it."

1 Titles

Match a title with a part of the story.

I think 'A rainy afternoon' is a good title for the … part of the story.

> Just like a film
>
> So boring!
>
> A dead woman?
>
> Water came through the windows and doors
>
> Helicopters arrived
>
> A rainy afternoon

2 An interview

After the disaster lots of reporters came to Boscastle. One reporter spoke to Kate.

a) *Act dialogues with a partner. One of you is the reporter. The other is Kate.*

A: Can I ask you some questions about the disaster in Boscastle?
B: Yes, of course.
A: Where were you …?
B: I can remember that quite well. I was … .

> Where were you when the disaster started?
>
> What was the worst …?
>
> What happened?
>
> Were you scared when …?
>
> How did you feel when the water …?
>
> How … your parents?

b) *Now write the interview.*

1 Parents and children

Children often have to help their parents. *Make sentences.*

1. you – help in the kitchen/I – cook your favourite meal
   If you help in the kitchen, I'll cook your favourite meal.
2. you – want a sandwich/I – make one for you
3. you – tidy up your room/we – watch a DVD together tonight
4. you – don't tidy up your room/we – watch it without you
5. you – don't do that Maths homework/your teacher – be angry
6. you – work hard for your Geography test/you – get a better grade
7. you …/I …

2 Speaking: No, thank you!

Kate and Susie/cook a curry

Simon/make a cake for a party

Lisa and Tom/repair Tom's bike

Ben/write his History project

Helen/book a flight

I	myself
you	yourself
he	himself
she	herself
we	ourselves
they	themselves

Make different dialogues.
You can act a dialogue like this: *or like this:*

A: What are Kate and Susie doing?   *A:* Hi, Kate. What are you doing?
B: They're cooking an Indian curry.   *B:* Hi. We're cooking a curry.
A: Should we help them?   *A:* Can I help you?
B: No. They can cook it themselves.   *B:* No, thank you. We can cook it ourselves.

3 Listening: Different people

Four different people are talking about
the Boscastle disaster.
*Who are the speakers? Which words tell
you? Take notes.*

1. First speaker: … . Words: …
2. *Go on, please.*

> a teacher
> somebody that has got a shop
> a reporter
> a taxi driver
> somebody that lives in the village
> a tourist

▷ **4** **A picture story**

Look at the pictures. Tell the story. Find your own ending.

One day in August, Sue Brown and her parents visited Boscastle.
They parked their car … .   *Go on, please.*

5 **The 'If . . .' game**

a) *Work in a group. Everybody writes the first part of a sentence with 'If …'.*
Give it to the next player, but he/she mustn't see the sentence.
This player finishes the sentence.

b) *Now read your sentences to the group.*

> If you give me 10 euros,
> - - - - - - - - - - - - - -
> **I'll push you into the river.**
> - - - - - - - - - - - - - -
> If you give me your phone,
> - - - - - - - - - - - - - -
> **I'll cook it for lunch.**

6 **Mediation: Fire**

You're in a hotel with a group of German tourists.
One of the tourists can't speak English and asks what this sign says.
Tell the tourist about the sign in German.

– Was sollte man zuerst tun, wenn es brennt?
– Sollte man zuerst seine Wertsachen holen?
– Wo sollte man hingehen?
– Sollte man zurückgehen?
– Was soll man dabei einschlagen?

Arbeiten mit dem Wörterbuch IV
Ein Wörterbuch kann sehr hilfreich sein. Aber Vorsicht! Nicht immer ist die erste englische Bedeutung die richtige! Schaue dir immer alle Bedeutungen an, bevor du dich für eine entscheidest.

Ein Beispiel: Du willst sagen, dass du vergessen hast, deinen Wecker zu stellen. Du wirst merken, dass „stellen" in deinem Wörterbuch ganz unterschiedliche Bedeutungen hat. Welche ist die richtige? Lies weiter und du findest in den meisten Wörterbüchern einen speziellen Eintrag zu deiner Frage, z.B. „den Wecker ~ set the alarm". Dein Satz heißt demnach „I forgot to set the alarm." Probier dasselbe einmal mit den markierten Wörtern aus. Welches ist die richtige Bedeutung?

1. Ich schlage ihn im Tennis immer.
(schlagen)
2. Er hat den Ball nicht getroffen.
(treffen)
3. Deine Hose sitzt gut.
(sitzen)

7 Word web: Weather

Make a word web for 'weather' in your exercise book.

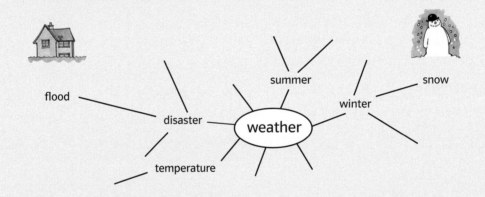

8 Weather friends

Find pairs.
1. rain – anoraks
2. *Go on, please.*

> anoraks • rain • tornado • degrees
> flood • summer • snow • too much water
> winter • temperature • warm • destroy

9 Listen and speak ◎

Read these sentences. Put the words with 'th' in two groups.

	[ð]	[θ]
1. Does **the** hot wea**th**er make you **th**irsty?		
2. **Th**ink of **th**ree **th**ings **th**at start with 'th'.		
3. **Th**row **th**ese Ma**th**s books into **th**e box. **Th**ank you.	the	thirsty
4. On **the** **th**ird **Th**ursday of **th**is mon**th**, fa**th**ers and mo**th**ers can see ano**th**er school play.	weather …	…

10 What's the weather like?

Talk about the weather.

1. The weather in London is sunny. The temperature is 24 degrees. That's warm!
2. The weather in Edinburgh is … .
   Go on, please.

☀	☁	🌧	🌧	☀	**?**
24°	17°	20°	18°	32°	?°
London	Edinburgh	Cardiff	Berlin	New York	Your town

11 The wrong word

What's the wrong word?

1. hot, busy, warm, cold
   The wrong word is 'busy'.
2. pilot, witch, teacher, caretaker
   Go on, please.
3. valley, mountain, coast, headline
4. fire, wind, rain, snow
5. car, helicopter, bus, van
6. storm, tornado, flood, cloudy
7. river, field, lake, sea
8. bad, high, wide, long

▷ 12 Let's go to Cornwall!

Some words are wrong here. What's right?

1. Let's go to Cornwall next **winter**.
   Let's go to Cornwall next summer.
2. The weather will be **cold** there.
   Go on, please.
3. We can stay at the **old** campsite.
4. The campsite is **more expensive** than a hotel.
5. It's got a **big** swimming pool.
6. We mustn't **remember** our tent!
7. We'll have a **bad** holiday.

13 A cartoon

It must be summer, the rain's warmer.

14 A poem: Bad weather ◎

a) *What's missing?*

I'm always upset
When it's cold and … .

It isn't funny
When it's too hot and … .

When there's snow
I think 'Oh, …!'

And when there's ice
It isn't … .

I almost never
Like the …!

b) *Listen and check your answers.*

poem – *Gedicht;* ice – *Eis*

If-clauses *(Bedingungssätze)*

Verwendung:
Du verwendest if-Sätze, um zu sagen,
unter welcher Bedingung etwas gesche-
hen wird.

If it rains, we**'ll need** our anoraks.
If it's sunny, we**'ll leave** them here.

Bildung:
Im Bedingungssatz mit if *steht das*
present simple, *im Hauptsatz das* will-
future.

If somebody **comes** with me, I**'ll go** to
the cinema tonight.
If we **don't go** now, we **won't be** there
on time.

Achtung!
Im Deutschen wird in Bedingungs-
sätzen nur die Gegenwart verwendet.

If they **stay** another week, I**'ll leave**!

Welcher Beispielsatz passt zu Cartoon A? Warum?

Reflexive pronouns *(Reflexivpronomen)*

Verwendung:
Du verwendest die Reflexivpronomen
- *um zu sagen, dass jemand etwas*
  selbst gemacht hat.
- *wie das deutsche Wort ‚sich'.*

I did it **myself**.

They tried to save **themselves**.

Bildung:
Singular: -self
Plural: -selves

I	→	my**self**	we	→	our**selves**
you	→	your**self**	you	→	your**selves**
he	→	him**self**	they	→	them**selves**
she	→	her**self**			

Welcher Beispielsatz passt zu Cartoon B? Warum?

Checklist

Ich kann		

Ich kann

... *über das Wetter sprechen.*
... *sagen, wie das Wetter werden wird.*
... *sagen, was ich mache, falls das Wetter schlecht wird.*
... *sagen, was ich mache, falls das Wetter gut wird.*
... *sagen, was ich immer selbst mache.*
... *sagen, was jemand für/mit sich selbst getan hat.*
... *von einem Ereignis berichten.*

The temperature is 38 degrees today!
There will be more rain next week.
If it rains again tomorrow, we won't stay here.
If the weather is better tomorrow, we'll go to the beach.
I always do my homework myself.
They tried to save themselves.

On August 16th there was a very bad storm in Boscastle.

Checkout: Help us to help the environment!

THE GREEN VILLAGE HOTEL

Dear guest,
Many tons of detergents and water are wasted every day to wash towels that have only been used for a short period of time. We would be grateful if you could help us to do something against this! Please help us to protect our environment by using your towels twice. Thank your very much for your help!
Have a pleasant stay!

The Green Village Hotel Management

If you want to use your towels again, just leave them on the towel rack.

If you want new towels, just put them on the floor in front of your door.

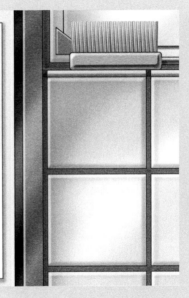

Was würdest du mit deinen Handtüchern machen?
Hier gibt es wie immer einige Wörter und Wendungen, die du nicht kennst. Du kannst sie aus dem Zusammenhang erschließen oder in der alphabetischen Wortliste ab S. 107 nachschlagen.

TIPP

Tipps: Help us to help the environment!
1. are wasted: *Dies ist eine Verbform im Passiv. Das heißt, es wird etwas mit einer Sache gemacht.*
2. by using: *Hier wird konkret vorgeschlagen, wie man helfen kann.*
3. towel, towel rack: *Versuche diese Wörter aus dem Zusammenhang zu erschließen. Du siehst sie auch auf den Bildern.*

Top sports

a We asked some young people about their favourite sports and activities. Here are their answers.

> I really like Formula One. I think it's a great spectator sport. I always watch the races when they're on TV. Formula One is really exciting, but it's also dangerous.

darts

Tim, London

> One of my friends plays chess. He wants to be a champion. I don't play chess, because it's boring. I prefer to be active and do something, like karate. My father plays darts. I don't think that's a sport.

Ashraf, Manchester

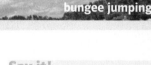
bungee jumping

chess

Say it!

It's exciting, but it's also dangerous.
I prefer to be active.

Es ist aufregend, aber auch gefährlich.
Ich bin lieber aktiv.

---

1 **Sports and activities**

a) *Think of sports and activities. Put them in these groups. Some sports and activities can go into more than one group.*

b) *Can you think of other groups for sports and activities?*

> **spectator sports**
> Formula One
> …

> **leisure activities**
> darts
> …

> **extreme sports**
> bungee jumping
> …

> **team sports**
> football
> …

karate

I don't like extreme sports. I don't know why people do them. They know that they could have an awful accident. My favourite sport is ice skating.

Helen, Abergavenny

Formula One

ice skating

2 Speaking: Your sports

Ask a partner.

A: What's your favourite spectator sport?
B: I like … because … .
A: Do you like extreme sports?
B: Yes, I do. I like … because … . /
   No, I don't. I hate them because … .

> spectator sports   leisure activities
>   extreme sports   team sports

▷ 3 Speaking: Sports results

Look at the sports page of a newspaper. What sports results can you find from the UK? Tell the class.

There was a … game / race / competition in … yesterday.
… won. …

b Are you an active type or are you a couch potato? Do you jump on a skateboard or do you sit in front of the TV in your free time? This quiz will show you how active you are.

A quiz

Which type are you?

1. You've got some free time. What do you do?
a) Listen to music and dance
b) Watch TV or play computer games
c) Do sports or go to training

2. How often do you do sports?
a) More than once a week
b) Once a week
c) Only at school

3. You're with a friend. What do you prefer to do?
a) Go where you can dance / talk
b) Go to the cinema
c) Go swimming

4. It's the weekend. Do you sleep until ...
a) 8 o'clock?
b) 9 o'clock?
c) 1 o'clock?

5. Which of these clubs would you like to join?
a) A club like the film club
b) A sports club where you're always active
c) A music club or an art club

6. Which of these questions can you always answer?
a) Did you / your team win the last game?
b) How did that detective story finish?
c) Who won the football game on TV?

7. You've got some money for your birthday. What would you like to buy?
a) New trainers
b) A new DVD, CD or computer game
c) A football, a basketball or a skateboard

8. Which of these holidays do you prefer?
a) A beach holiday where you can swim
b) An activity holiday with lots of sport
c) A holiday where you can be very lazy

4 Active type or couch potato?

Check your partner's answers. Tell him / her about the results.

How many points?			You can say:
1. a) 5	b) 0	c) 10	55–80 points: Congratulations! You're very active. You enjoy sports.
2. a) 10	b) 5	c) 0	
3. a) 5	b) 0	c) 10	
4. a) 10	b) 5	c) 0	30–50 points: You're quite active. But you could do more sports.
5. a) 0	b) 10	c) 5	
6. a) 10	b) 0	c) 5	5–25 points: You really should be more active.
7. a) 5	b) 0	c) 10	
8. a) 5	b) 10	c) 0	0 points: That's a pity! You really are a couch potato!

5 Popular sports

a) Here are the results of a survey about sports that people do in the UK. *What's missing?*

1. … is the most popular sport.
2. … go swimming.
3. … do yoga and … .
4. … isn't very popular. Only … do that.

Which sports have you done this year?

walking: 46 %

swimming: 35 %

yoga and dance: 22 %

darts: 3 %

% = percent

b) *Find a survey like this for Germany. Are different sports popular?*

6 Listening with DJ Dan: Which sports?

Dan and his callers are talking about sports.
What do Gemma, Ben, Nicky and Scott do? Take notes.

	Gemma	Ben	…
sport?	tennis	…	
when?	every Tuesday	…	
where?	…		
how good?			

7 Writing: Your favourite activity

Write about your favourite sport or leisure activity. First make notes.

– What's your favourite sport or activity?
– How often do you do it?
– Do you go to a club?

– Are you in a team?
– Do you go to training? If you go to training, when?
– Have you ever won anything?

8 A song: We are the champions

Mercury, Freddy

I've paid my dues, time after time.
I've done my sentence,
But committed no crime.
And bad mistakes,
I've made a few,
I've had my share of sand
Kicked in my face,
But I've come through.

We are the champions, my friends,
And we'll keep on fighting till the end.
We are the champions,
We are the champions,
No time for losers,
'Cause we are the champions
Of the world.

dues – *Lehrgeld*; time after time – *immer wieder*; do my sentence – *meine Strafe absitzen*; commit – *begehen*; crime – *Verbrechen*; mistake – *Fehler*; a few – *ein paar*; share – *Anteil*; sand – *Sand*; I've come through – *ich habe es geschafft*; we'll keep on fighting – *wir werden weiterkämpfen*; till – *bis*; loser – *Verliererin, Verlierer*; 'cause – *weil*; world – *Welt*

Project: Sports clubs

Work in groups. Write a profile of a sports club you know and present it to the class. You can make a poster or a presentation. Here are some ideas for your work:

- What do you know about the history of the club? How old is it?
- What's the sport like? Is it dangerous, extreme, popular, boring? Can you show the sport to the class?
- Is it difficult to join the club? How many people are in the club? How much does it cost?
- Has the club got any famous players? Which competitions has the club won?
- Do you like the club and the sport? Why or why not?

As always, organize your work in four steps:

1. *Plan the work! (Which club? Who does what?)*
2. *Do the work! (Find information and pictures, write texts and make a poster.)*
3. *Present the work! (Show your poster to the class or give your presentation.)*
4. *Talk about the project! (What was good? What can you do better next time?)*

So easy for Greenwich

More than 300 people watched Greenwich Hockey Club walk to a very easy 4-0 win in their home game against East Ham on Saturday.

Greenwich Hockey Club: Champions of England!

Greenwich Hockey Club won their tenth game of the season on Saturday and are now champions of England. They have played great hockey since Christmas.

Greenwich Hockey Club

About us
News and Events
Coaches
Team
Summer Camp
Home

WELCOME to the website of Greenwich Hockey Club!

Checklist

Ich kann	
... sagen, dass etwas aufregend, aber gefährlich ist.	It's exciting, but dangerous.
... sagen, dass ich eine bestimmte Sportart immer schaue.	I always watch Formula One on TV.
... sagen, was mir lieber ist.	I prefer to be active.
... jemandem gratulieren.	Congratulations!
... jemanden fragen, ob er Sport treibt.	Do you do sports?
... jemanden nach seinem Lieblingssport fragen.	What's your favourite sport?
... jemanden fragen, wie oft er einen Sport betreibt.	How often do you go swimming?

U1 London
U2 Handy
U3 Wales
U4 Schule
U5 Schottland
U6 Musik
U7 Wetter
U8 Sport

Strategy: Listening ◎

Das Hören von englischen Texten kann man üben. Die folgenden Tipps können dir dabei helfen. Probiere sie mit dem Text ‚Gemma and Helen on the phone' aus, den du auf der CD im Workbook findest.

A Vor dem Hören

- *Mache dir klar, um was für eine Art von Text es sich handelt (ist es z.B. ein Telefongespräch, ein Fernsehbericht oder eine Erzählung?).*
- *Finde heraus, wer mit wem über was spricht.*
- *Überlege, was du über das Thema bereits weißt und was du von dem Text erwartest.*

B Während des ersten Hörens

- *Mache dir keine Notizen, entspanne dich und höre einfach nur konzentriert zu!*
- *Sorge für grundsätzliche Orientierung: Was passiert wo, wann und mit welchen Personen?*

C Während des zweiten Hörens

- *Mache dir Notizen in einem Hörprotokoll:*

Wer?	Was?	Warum?	Wann?	Wo?
Gemma and Helen	...	...	...	...

D Nach dem Hören

- *Fasse den Text mündlich für eine Freundin oder einen Freund zusammen. Du kannst das auf Englisch oder Deutsch tun.*
- *Falls es Fragen zum Text gibt, kannst du diese jetzt beantworten.*

Grammar

1 Questions and answers

Match the questions with the answers.

1. When do you want to go to Scotland? — We'd like to stay in a cottage.
2. How can I get to Scotland?   I totally love DJ Dan!
3. What would you like to do there?   Well, I like darts.
4. Where would you like to stay?   → We'll go there in late August.
5. Have you ever been to London?   If it's sunny, we'll go swimming.
6. Who's your favourite DJ?   You can take a flight.
7. What will you do at the weekend?   Yes, we went there last year.
8. What's your favourite sport?   We'd like to climb Ben Nevis.

2 We haven't done it yet!

Make sentences.

1. we / not / book / the hotel / yet
   We haven't booked the hotel yet.
2. Tom / not / be / to London / yet   *Go on, please.*
3. look, I / find / some money / in street
4. sorry, / I / just / break / Grandma's expensive cup
5. we / not / see / Nessie / yet
6. sorry, I / not / do / my homework / yet

3 Myself, yourself, …

myself/yourself   himself/herself   ourselves/yourselves/themselves

What's missing?

1. Why don't you make your bed …, Tom?
   Why don't you make your bed yourself, Tom?
2. I can't make it … today. I haven't got time.   *Go on, please.*
3. Sally always does her Maths homework … . Tim never does his homework … .
4. Andrew's parents cook all the meals at the Ness House … .
5. Can we help you? – No, thank you, we can repair the bikes … .
6. Why don't you tidy up your rooms …, Cathy and Ken?

4 If …

Make sentences.

1. If she (leave) me, I (be) sad.
   If she leaves me, I'll be sad.
2. If it (be) sunny tomorrow, we (go) swimming.   *Go on, please.*
3. But if it (rain), we (not go) to the beach.
4. If Tom (not train) more, he (lose) the next race, too.
5. If you (not visit) us this evening, I (not see) you again before the holidays.

Words

5 Peter Robbins

What's the best word?

song	loudly	voice	play	download	important		orchestra
internet	practise	nervous	meet	singer	listen to		understands

Hello, my name is Peter Robbins.
I … the trumpet in our school … . We have to … every week. At home I mustn't play too … because that makes my sister … .
My girlfriend Ashley is a … . She's got a great … . At weekends we often … . We … CDs or … music from the … . Ashley really … me.
Music is very … for us! Our favourite … is 'We are the champions'.

6 Andrew

a) *Which letters are missing? Write the sentences again.*

Andrew *lw*ys w*tch*s F*rm*l* *n* r*c*s *n TV.
Th*y *r* r**lly *xc*t*ng, b*t *ls* v*ry d*ng*r**s.

b) *Make an exercise for your partner. Write a sentence from Units 5-8 without a, e, i, o and u. Your partner must write the sentence again with the right letters.*

7 What is it?

Say what the words mean in English.

1. sight: This is a famous place.
2. download   *Go on, please.*
3. couch potato
4. loch
5. bed and breakfast
6. trombone
7. snow

This is a … .   This means that … .
This is somebody that … .
You can see this in … .
This is a place where … .
With a … you can … .   This is the same as … .
This is another word for … .

8 A presentation

Do a short presentation on one of these topics. Make notes first.

My music	Scotland	Sports
favourite band	towns and cities	favourite sport
favourite song	famous places	sports type
favourite style of music	sights	active/couch potato
CDs	nature	clubs
posters	places to stay	training
download	weather	favourite sports star
instrument	people	favourite club

Mediation

Englisch brauchst du nicht nur, um mit Engländern, Amerikanern oder Australiern zu sprechen. Du brauchst es auch, um Leuten zu helfen, die nicht so gut Englisch können. Dann kann es sein, dass du vermitteln oder übersetzen musst. Oft kann es auch passieren, dass du englische Informationen auf Deutsch weitergeben musst. All dies kannst du in den Aufgaben auf dieser Doppelseite üben.

1 Zwei Londoner Sehenswürdigkeiten (nach Unit 1)

Du bist mit deiner Klasse auf Klassenfahrt in London. In der Touristeninformation habt ihr euch einige Faltblätter von Londoner Sehenswürdigkeiten besorgt. *Arbeite mit einem Partner zusammen. Jeder von euch liest einen der beiden Texte. Erzähle deinem Partner anschließend auf Deutsch, was deine Sehenswürdigkeit so besonders macht. Überlegt dann gemeinsam, wohin ihr gehen möchtet.*

INFORMATION

TOWER OF LONDON

Go back in time at the Tower of London! The Tower is almost 1000 years old. First it was a castle for the English king. Then a part of it was an awful prison[1] for the people the king didn't like. You can see the crown jewels[2] here and the place where King Henry VIII killed[3] his second wife[4]!

The Underground station is Tower Hill. Tickets are £11.50 (children: £7.50).

MADAME TUSSAUD'S

Would you like to meet Robbie Williams, Arnold Schwarzenegger or Boris Becker? No problem! Visit Madame Tussaud's and meet many famous people there. See your favourite sports stars or stand next to your favourite actor[5]. Don't forget your camera[6] – you can take photos! Your friends at home won't see that all the famous people are really wax figures[7]...

The Underground station is Baker Street. Tickets are £9.50 (children: £6.50).

[1] prison – *Gefängnis*; [2] crown jewels – *Kronjuwelen*; [3] kill – *ermorden, töten*; [4] wife – *Ehefrau*; [5] actor – *Schauspieler, Schauspielerin*; [6] camera – *Fotoapparat*; [7] wax figures – *Wachsfiguren*

2 Loch Ness bei Nacht

(nach Unit 5)

Du bist in einem Souvenirgeschäft in Schottland. Eine deutsche Frau sucht nach einem Geschenk für ihren Sohn. Sie kann kein Englisch und weiß nicht, was sie sagen soll, als der Verkäufer sie anspricht. Kannst du ihr helfen?
Arbeite mit zwei Partnern zusammen, die den Verkäufer und die Frau spielen.

Verkäufer:	Can I help you?
Frau:	Wie bitte? Oh je, ich suche ein Geschenk für meinen Sohn.
Du:	(zu der Frau) Kann ich Ihnen helfen? (zu dem Verkäufer)…
Verkäufer:	A present for her son? Does he know about Loch Ness and Nessie?
Du:	…
Frau:	Ja, aber er findet Nessie langweilig. Er glaubt nicht, dass es hier ein Monster gibt.
Du:	…
Verkäufer:	Hm, that's funny. How old is he? Does he like T-shirts with castles on them? We've got some new ones with new designs.
Du:	…
Frau:	Er ist 13 und trägt nur schwarze Klamotten, weil er sie cool findet.
Du:	…
Verkäufer:	I've got an idea. We've got very cool black T-shirts with 'Loch Ness by night' on them. Look here.
Du:	…
Frau:	Das ist eine gute Idee. Wie viel kosten sie?
Du:	…
Verkäufer:	One T-shirt is £10, but you can get two for £15.
Du:	…
Frau:	Super! Dann nehme ich zwei.
Du:	…

3 Im Schilderwald

(nach Unit 8)

Eine Fußballmannschaft aus Italien ist zu Gast bei eurem Sportverein. Ihr könnt euch nur auf Englisch mit ihnen unterhalten. Auf Ausflügen fragen sie immer wieder nach Dingen, die sie nicht verstehen. *Erkläre ihnen diese Schilder:*

It means that ….
You mustn't ….
You must ….
You can only ….

One country – or four?

The British Isles[1]

The countries of **Great Britain**[2] are England, Wales and Scotland.

The countries of **the United Kingdom** (UK) are Great Britain (England, Wales, Scotland) and Northern Ireland[3].

The countries of **the British Isles** are the UK and the Republic of Ireland[4].

 = the British Isles

1 How many?

1. How many countries are there in the United Kingdom? What are their names?
2. Which country is in the UK but isn't a part of Great Britain?
3. Which country is in the British Isles but isn't in the UK?
4. Which is the biggest country in the British Isles?

2 Find it!

Look at the map at the front of your book.

1. London is the capital[5] of England and the UK. Find the capitals of Wales, Scotland, Northern Ireland and the Republic of Ireland.
2. Find mountains in Scotland and Wales.
3. Find a river in the Republic of Ireland.
4. Find the part of England where there are lots of lakes.
5. Find the tunnel between the UK and France.

3 England – English

Make a list. Use your dictionary for other countries.

England	Wales	Russia
Italy	the UK/Great Britain	
Germany	Ireland	France
Turkey	Scotland	...

Irish	Turkish	French
Scottish	Welsh	English
British	Russian	German
Italian	...	

England – English
Wales – ...

---

[1]the British Isles – *die britischen Inseln*; [2]Great Britain – *Großbritannien*; [3]Northern Ireland – *Nordirland*; [4]the Republic of Ireland – *Irland*; [5]capital – *Hauptstadt*

◎ A dangerous place

Let's go back in time. It's the year 1600 and we're in London.

London is the biggest city in England. There are lots of people in the streets. Every day it's like a big theatre[1]: music, clowns, animals and food everywhere[2]. Men, women and children sell things in the streets. It's very loud because everybody shouts and the animals make lots of noise, too.

London is very dirty[3]. Most houses haven't got toilets or bathrooms. People throw their dirty water and rubbish[4] through their windows into the street. So if you aren't careful, something will fall on your head! People on the road to London can smell[5] the town from fifteen kilometres away. It stinks[6] awfully!

The streets are dark at night and there are many robbers[7] in London. So you should stay at home in the evening. But during the day it can also be very dangerous because there are lots of people, dogs, horses, cows and sheep on the roads. There are no police officers in London. People can run through the streets, break windows or start fires! Almost no children go to school, so not many people can read or write. Girls can't go to school. There are some famous boys' schools in London – but they are only for boys from rich[8] families.

1 A text for the school magazine

Write a text about old London for your school magazine.

London was the biggest city in England. There were lots of people in the streets. Every day was like a big theatre: …

2 Would you like to live there?

Would you like to live in old London? *Say why or why not.*

Yes, I would because … .
No, I wouldn't because … .

> no schools   smelly   dirty   dangerous   fun
> like a big theatre   no toilets   no police   no cars

[1]theatre – *Theater*; [2]everywhere – *überall*; [3]dirty – *dreckig*; [4]rubbish – *Abfall*; [5]smell – *riechen*; [6]stink – *stinken*; [7]robber – *Räuber*; [8]rich – *reich*

Andrew's photos

We're picking up[1] the campervan[2] from the Bensons. My sisters aren't too happy about it, but I think it's OK.

This is my room. I always leave things until the last minute. How can I get everything into one rucksack?

We're almost ready to leave. I've just put a little surprise for my sisters in one of the beds.

Let's go! Mum is driving and Dad is reading the map. We go round and round[3] for an hour before we leave London.

We stopped here for a sandwich. A typical[4] English castle.

All the campsites are full. It's raining and raining. Our campervan hasn't got a toilet. Help!

We've decided to camp in this field. Let's hope nobody sees us. Water is coming into the campervan. Dad is trying to find the hole. Mum is shouting at him.

The next morning, Dad has repaired the hole, but we can't make tea or cook our food because there aren't any matches[5].
Dad is trying to start a fire with two sticks[6]. Mum is laughing.

We got some food in a fantastic fun park. But I'm not sure if Dad liked it. His famous last words before he got on: "Maybe I shouldn't eat a third hot dog!"

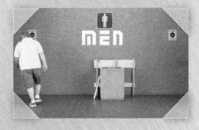

Then we didn't see him for an hour.

Cycling[7] and walking in Wales can be fun. But my bike has got a flat tyre[8] AGAIN! And all this healthy activity is too much for Mum.

"I know a faster and shorter way," Dad said on one of our walking trips. I've never seen so many sheep.

A 'traditional[9] English breakfast' — in a Welsh B&B! Fried[10] bacon[11], fried eggs, fried sausages[12], and toast. Mum calls it a 'heart attack[13] on a plate[14]'.

Three days without photos — no film in the camera!

The Jones' new house in Penryn. The campervan isn't working again, but they say that we can stay with them as long as we like!!! So Mum gets her 'hotel', Dad can relax, and the Jones have given me their tent. We go swimming and surfing every day, so it's a perfect[15] holiday!

1 How fast can you find them?

Work with a partner. Read the texts and see how fast you can find:

| three animals | six things to eat | four places to sleep | four hobbies |

▷ 2 Your holiday story

Write about a funny, fantastic or terrible holiday. It can be something that really happened or you can write a new story. If you want, you can also use photos.

[1]campervan – *Wohnmobil*; [2]pick up – *abholen*; [3]round and round – *im Kreis*; [4]typical – *typisch*; [5]matches – *Streichhölzer*; [6]stick – *Stock*; [7]cycling – *Fahrrad fahren*; [8]have a flat tyre – *einen Platten haben*; [9]traditional – *traditionell*; [10]fried – *gebraten*; [11]bacon – *Schinkenspeck*; [12]sausage – *Wurst, Würstchen*; [13]heart attack – *Herzinfarkt*; [14]plate – *Teller*; [15]perfect – *perfekt*

Three poems

1 Films Swimming ool

Swimming in the swimming pool
is where I like to 'B',
wearing underwater goggles[1]
so that I can 'C'.

Yesterday, before I swam,
I drank a cup of 'T'.
Now the pool's a 'swimming ool'
because I took a 'P'[2].

Kenn Nesbitt

*The letters at the end
of every second line are
really words. Can you
write the words?*

*Find more English words
that you can write as a
letter or number. Can you
write a poem with them?*

2 Films

Some films are sad – you watch them and cry[3].
You know that the hero[4] is going to die.
Some films have spies[5] – they fight, run and jump.
When they crash[6] their cars, there's a very big bump[7]!
Sometimes aliens[8] come down from space[9].
That often means trouble for the human race[10].
And then there are ghost films – ghosts come out at night
And give everybody an awful fright[11].
But the worst films are love films where all the stars kiss[12].
Those are the films that I want to miss!

William Sears

3 Lucky trade[13]

I told my mum I'd go to work
if she would go to school.
She thought that trading places[14] once
just might be kind of[15] cool.

So she agreed[16]; I packed her lunch
and made her wash her face.
Then mother said, "I wonder[17] why
you want to take my place?"

"I wonder what you do at work.
I'd like to meet your boss.
Now hurry up[18] and brush[19] your teeth[20]
and don't forget to floss[21].

There's just one other thing, Mom, that I
forgot to mention[22].
I'll pick you up at four o'clock
because today you have detention."

Matthew Fredericks

[1] goggles – *Schwimmbrille*; [2] take a pee – *pinkeln*; [3] cry – *weinen*; [4] hero – *Held/Heldin*; [5] spies – *Spione*; [6] crash – *verunglücken*; [7] bump – *Zusammenstoß*; [8] aliens – *Außerirdische*; [9] space – *das Weltall*; [10] human race – *die Menschheit*; [11] fright – *Schreck*; [12] kiss – *küssen*; [13] lucky trade – *guter Tausch*; [14] trading places – *Plätze tauschen, Rollen tauschen*; [15] kind of – *irgendwie*; [16] agree – *zustimmen*; [17] wonder – *sich wundern*; [18] hurry up – *sich beeilen*; [19] brush – *bürsten, putzen*; [20] teeth – *Zähne*; [21] floss – *Zahnseide verwenden*; [22] mention – *erwähnen*

Vocabulary

Auf den *Vocabulary*-Seiten findest du alle Wörter und Wendungen in der Reihenfolge, in der sie in *Let's go 3* vorkommen. In der linken Spalte steht das englische Wort, in der Mitte die deutsche Übersetzung und rechts ein Beispielsatz, eine Abbildung oder eine Sammelbox. Wenn du wissen willst, wie ein Wort ausgesprochen wird, schaust du in der *Alphabetical word list* ab S. 107 nach. Dort findest du alle Wörter aus *Let's go* in alphabetischer Reihenfolge und mit der Lautschrift, die dir sagt, wie die Wörter ausgesprochen werden. Hier ist eine Liste der wichtigsten Lautschriftzeichen.

Englische Laute (English sounds)

Selbstlaute (Vowels)

[ɑː]	car; ähnlich wie in *Bahn*
[ʌ]	number; ähnlich wie in *Dach*
[e]	yes; ähnlich wie in *nett*
[ə]	a pen; ähnlich wie der Endlaut in *bitte*
[ɜː]	girl
[æ]	bag
[ɪ]	it; ähnlich wie in *Kind*
[i]	happy; ähnlich wie in *Gummi*
[iː]	see; ähnlich wie in *tief*
[ɒ]	on; ähnlich wie in *Kopf*
[ɔː]	morning; ähnlich wie in *ohne*
[ʊ]	put; ähnlich wie in *Schutt*
[uː]	you; ähnlich wie in *du*

Doppellaute (Diphthongs)

[aɪ]	my; ähnlich wie in *kein*
[aʊ]	now; ähnlich wie in *Frau*
[eə]	there
[eɪ]	say
[ɪə]	here
[ɔɪ]	boy; ähnlich wie in *Heu*
[əʊ]	go
[ʊə]	tourist

Mitlaute (Consonants)

[j]	yes; wie das deutsche *j* in *ja*
[l]	school
[ŋ]	song
[r]	ruler
[s]	see; stimmloses ‚s' wie in *reißen*
[z]	is, stimmhaftes ‚s' wie in *brausen*
[ʒ]	television; wie in *Jalousie* und *Gelee*
[dʒ]	jeans; wie in *Dschungel*
[ʃ]	she; wie in *Tisch*
[tʃ]	teacher; wie in *deutsch*
[ð]	this; stimmhafter Lispellaut
[θ]	thank you; stimmloser Lispellaut
[v]	video; wie in *Wasser*
[w]	what

[ː]	bedeutet, dass der vorangehende Laut lang ist, z. B. you [juː]
[']	bedeutet, dass die folgende Silbe betont ist, z. B. hello [hə'ləʊ]

Das englische Alphabet (The English alphabet)

a	[eɪ]	b	[biː]	c	[siː]	d	[diː]	e	[iː]
f	[ef]	g	[dʒiː]	h	[eitʃ]	i	[aɪ]	j	[dʒeɪ]
k	[keɪ]	l	[el]	m	[em]	n	[en]	o	[əʊ]
p	[piː]	q	[kjuː]	r	[ɑː]	s	[es]	t	[tiː]
u	[juː]	v	[viː]	w	['dʌbljuː]	x	[eks]		
y	[waɪ]	z	[zed]						

Unit 1: London

8	**Notting Hill Carnival**	*(Karneval im Londoner Stadteil Notting Hill)*	
	carnival	Karneval, Volksfest	
	during	während →	We mustn't eat *during* lessons at school.
	Tower of London	*(Zitadelle in London)*	
	king	König →	
	queen	Königin →	She's the *queen* and he's the *king*.
	for ... years	... Jahre lang →	We lived in London *for 5 years*, from 1998 to 2003.
	hundreds	hunderte, viele hundert	
	Buckingham Palace	*(Wohnsitz der britischen Königin)*	

> **A special family**
> father = **king**
> mother = **queen**
> daughter = **princess**
> son = **prince**

	palace	Palast →	A king or queen lives in a *palace*.
	uncle	Onkel →	Your dad's brother is your *uncle*.
	sight	Sehenswürdigkeit →	A *sight* is a famous or interesting place.
	dialogue	Dialog, Gespräch	
9	**Hindu**	hinduistisch; Hindu	
	temple	Tempel →	Indian people don't usually go to a church. They go to a *temple*.

> **Where would you like to live?**
> In a house or a flat or ...
> a church,
> a temple,
> a palace,
> a tower,
> a castle?

	wedding	Hochzeit →	People marry at a *wedding*.
	excited	aufgeregt, begeistert →	I'm very *excited* because we're going to visit an exciting place.
	West End	*(Stadtteil von London)*	
	notes	Notizen →	Don't write down all the information. Just *take notes*.
	take notes	Notizen machen →	
	list	Liste →	What must we do for our project? – Let's make a *list*.
	class	Schulklasse, Klasse →	*class* = tutor group

Language

10	**London Eye**	*(das größte Riesenrad der Welt)*	
	free	kostenlos, frei →	It's *free*. Don't pay for it.
	miss	vermissen, verpassen, verfehlen	
	What's missing?	Was fehlt?	
11	**ought to**	sollte besser/sollten besser →	You *ought to* get a bigger bike.

late	spät, zu spät →	Sorry I'm *late*.
sentence	Satz	

Text: Let's go to the carnival!

12	**West Indian**	westindisch; Westin-der/Westinderin →

The *West Indian* countries are between North and South America.

> **West Indian food isn't Indian food!**
> Es kommt nicht aus Indien, sondern von den 'West Indies'. Das sind kleine Inseln in der Karibik zwischen Nord- und Südamerika.

change to	umsteigen nach →	Take this bus to the market, then *change to* a number 29.
line	Linie, Zeile →	All the trains on this *line* go to Oxford Circus.
on the train	im Zug	
station	Haltestelle, Bahnhof →	Don't *get off* the train until it arrives at a *station*.
phone	Telefon →	*phone* = telephone
get off	aussteigen →	

> **London by Underground**
> Go to the **station**.
> Buy a **ticket**.
> Find the right **line**.
> **Get on** the train.
> **Get off** the train.
> **Change to** another line.

13	**Piccadilly Circus**	*(Platz in London)*
	demonstration	Demonstration
	Trafalgar Square	*(Platz in London)*
	may	dürfen, können →
	credit	Guthaben, Kredit →
	rang	klingelte/klingelten, läutete/läuteten
	order	Reihenfolge

May I open the window?
I can't phone Emily because I've got no *credit*.

Practice

14	**trip**	Fahrt, Reise
	German	deutsch; Deutscher/ Deutsche →

Kevin is *German*, and he speaks *German*. But he hasn't got a *German* name.

15	**tip**	Ratschlag, Tipp
	match	zuordnen →
	closed	geschlossen
	unit	Kapitel
	at the front	vorne
	Big Ben	*(Glockenturm des englischen Parlamentsgebäudes)*

When you *match* things, you put them together.

> **Can you match the sights and the pictures?**
>
> Big Ben
> Tower of London
> London Eye
> Piccadilly Circus
> Trafalgar Square

	mediation	Sprachmittlung →	In *mediation* exercises you help somebody when they can't understand or speak English.

Words

16	web	Netz, Netzwerk	
	dictionary	Wörterbuch	
17	go together	zusammenpassen	
	magazine	Zeitschrift, Magazin →	Jack is a sports fan, so he reads sports *magazines*.
	puzzle	Rätsel	

Lerncheck Unit 1

Welche Wörter fehlen?　　　　　carnival　magazine　sight　station　wedding

1. You can buy tickets for the train at the … .
2. Buckingham Palace is a famous … in London.
3. Hundreds of people go to the … and watch the processions.
4. This … has got lots of information about events in London.
5. Jenny went to her uncle's … last Saturday.

Unit 2:　It's good to talk!

20	topic	Thema	
	Is that you?	Bist du es?	
	It's me.	Ich bin's.	
	It's Barbara.	Hier ist Barbara.	
	text	eine SMS schreiben →	Please *text* me. = Please send me a text message.
	UK (United Kingdom)	Vereinigtes Königreich	
	penny pl. **pence**	Pence *(britische Währungseinheit)* →	1p = one *penny*. 10p = 10 *pence*.
	per	pro →	
	minute	Minute →	30p *per minute* = One minute costs 30p. ⚠ 'Minute' reimt sich mit 'win it'.
	mobile	Handy →	*mobile* = mobile phone
	network	Netz, Netzwerk →	Which *network* does your mobile phone use?
	phone call	Telefongespräch, Anruf →	When you phone somebody, you make a *phone call*.
	plan	Programm	
	bill	Rechnung →	I've got a phone *bill* for £50. Can you *pay* the *bill* please, Dad?
	pay, paid, paid	zahlen, bezahlen →	

> **Money, money, money**
> This shop **sells** mobile phones.
> You can **buy** mobiles here.
> They **cost** a lot of money.
> You must **pay** the **bill** for your phone calls.

	click	klicken	
	ring tone	Klingelton →	Do you like my new *ring tone*?

page	Seite	
add	addieren, hinzufügen →	When you *add* 1 and 2, you get 3.
as	während, als →	Tara always phones her friends *as* she walks along the road.
21 **Speak to you later.**	Bis dann. →	*Speak to you later.* = We can talk again another time.

phone box	Telefonzelle	
22 **switch off**	ausschalten →	Remember to *switch off* the radio when you go out.
steal, **stole**, **stolen**	stehlen	

> **Phones**
> You make a **phone call**.
> You download **ring tones**.
> You **switch off** your mobile in lessons.
> You phone from a **phone box** when your mobile isn't working.
> **Short forms**
> phone = telephone   mobile = mobile phone

23 **be wrong**	Unrecht haben →	This is Kate's laptop. – No, you*'re wrong*. It isn't Kate's, it's Nina's.
swim, **swam**, **swum**	schwimmen →	Mark is a good swimmer. He often *swims* for more than an hour.
ending	Ende, Schluss	

Project: Communication

24 **communication**	Kommunikation →	⚠ Die vorletzte Silbe wird betont.
way	Art, Weg, Methode →	That's not the best *way* to eat an apple.
history	Geschichte	
future	Zukunft →	⚠ Die erste Silbe wird betont. Sie reimt sich mit 'new'.
presentation	Präsentation →	We've got lots of information for our *presentation* to the class.

> **How to say it right**
> Keine Angst vor der Aussprache!
> Bei Wörtern, die mit **'-tion'** enden, wird die vorletzte Silbe betont:
> communi**ca**tion   presen**ta**tion
> infor**ma**tion   invi**ta**tion
> regis**tra**tion   au**di**tion
> compe**ti**tion   exhi**bi**tion

in English	auf Englisch	
25 **strategy**	Strategie, Lerntechnik	

Lerncheck Unit 2

Kannst du Mini-Dialoge zusammenstellen? Ein Satz aus A passt zu einem Satz aus B.

A	**B**
Sorry, I must stop now.	Yes, it is. Hi, Ben.
Emma, is that you?	I haven't got any credit.
Why can't you text your mum?	I'm sorry, I'll switch it off.
How much was your last phone bill?	OK, speak to you later.
You mustn't use your mobile here.	I can't remember. My dad paid it.

Unit 3: Wales

26	**Wales**	*(Halbinsel im Westen Großbritanniens)*	
	twinned	verschwistert →	Lots of German towns are *twinned* with towns in the UK.
	Abergavenny	*(kleine Stadt in Wales)*	
	trombone	Posaune →	She's playing the *trombone*.
	welcome	willkommen	
	Welsh	walisisch; Waliser/Wali-serin →	Wales is a country in the UK. People there speak the *Welsh language*.
	language	Sprache →	

Country	Language	Find out the names of …
Wales	Welsh/English	two **Welsh** towns.
England	English	three **English** football players.
Germany	German	four **German** castles.

27	**coal mine**	Kohlenbergwerk, Kohlengrube →	There are still some *coal mines* in Germany.
	Manchester United	*(bekannter englischer Fußballclub)*	
	against	gegen →	In this competition we must play *against* seven different teams.

Language

28	**training**	Training →	Football players have *training* every week, and the *coach* is their teacher.
	coach	Trainer →	
	concert	Konzert	

Sports and music

Simon **does sport**.	Nina **plays music**.
He **plays** football.	She **plays the** trombone.
… basketball.	… **the** drums.
… tennis.	… **the** guitar.
He **trains/has training** every day/week.	She **practises** every day/week.
His **coach** watches him.	Her **teacher** listens to her.
He plays in a **team**.	She plays in a **band/group**.
They have **games** against other teams.	They give **concerts**.

---

	last night	gestern Abend, gestern Nacht →	*last night* = yesterday evening
	this afternoon	heute Nachmittag →	Did you go jogging *this afternoon*? I phoned you but you weren't there.
	forget, forgot, forgotten	vergessen →	Please remember our concert next week. – OK, I won't *forget* it.
29	**Big Pit**	*(Bergbaumuseum in Wales)*	
	pit	Grube, Mine →	*Pit* is another word for 'coal mine'.
	miner	Bergarbeiter/Bergar-beiterin →	A *miner* works in a coal mine.
	grandad	Opa →	Your *grandad* is your father's or your mother's father.

tonight	heute Abend, heute Nacht →	We're going to a concert *tonight*. It starts at eight o'clock.

Yesterday	today
yesterday morning	this morning
yesterday afternoon	this afternoon
yesterday evening	this evening
aber:	
last night	**tonight**

mine	Mine	

Text: Katja and Rhodri

30	knew	wusste/wussten
	Carmarthen Castle	*(Burgruine in Carmarthen)*
	Carmarthen	*(Stadt im Südwesten von Wales)*
	thought	dachte/dachten
	watch	Armbanduhr →
	before	bevor →
	feel, felt, felt	fühlen, sich fühlen →
	well	gut →

a clock *a watch*

You should think carefully *before* you buy a pet.
How do you *feel*? – I *feel* very ill.
Rhodri is a good player.
He plays *well*.

How you can feel			
Sometimes you **feel** well.		Sometimes you **feel** ill.	
...	great.	...	awful.
...	good.	...	bad.
...	fantastic.	...	sad.

31	the next morning	am nächsten Morgen →	Last Friday Tim went to a great party. But *the next morning* he felt very tired.
	greeting	Gruß	

Practice

32	tour	Führung, Tour →	How long is the *tour* of the castle? – It's two hours long.
33	position	Platz, Position →	At the end of the competition our team was in the third *position*.
	point	Punkt →	When you win a football game, you get three *points*.
	away game	Auswärtsspiel →	Oxford played against Greenwich in Oxford. For the Oxford
	home game	Heimspiel →	team it was a *home game*. For Greenwich it was an *away game*.

Lerncheck Unit 3

Welche Wörter fehlen?   position   well   forgets   grandad   before

1. Luke always goes to Newtown's home games. He never .... .
2. He meets his friends ... the game starts.
3. Luke says, "Our team is in a good ... after the first five games."
4. He always sleeps ... after a good game.
5. Luke's ... played for Newtown forty years ago.

Unit 4: Is school cool?

38	**already**	schon, bereits	
39	**profile**	*(Zeugnis mit Selbstbeurteilung)* →	⚠ Das Wort *profile* reimt sich mit 'mobile'.
	be interested in	interessiert sein an, sich interessieren für →	I'*m interested in* music. = I think music is interesting.
	quite	ziemlich, ganz →	This book isn't fantastic. But it's *quite* good.
	report	Zeugnis, Bericht →	German pupils get their *reports* on the last day of the school year.
40	**detention**	Nachsitzen, Haft →	Let's go swimming after school. – I can't. I've got a *detention*.
	bully	tyrannisieren, drangsalieren →	The younger pupils are scared of Jack because he *bullies* them.
	sanction	Sanktion, Strafe	
	headteacher	Rektor/Rektorin, Schulleiter/Schulleiterin →	The *headteacher* is the most important teacher in a school.

> **New 'school' words**
> class
> profile
> headteacher
> detention
> sanction

	extra	zusätzlich; Zusatz →	Can I have *extra* chips, please?
41	**break, broke, broken**	brechen, zerbrechen →	Yesterday Ben *broke* a window. He *broke* a school rule, too!
	situation	Situation, Lage	
	wall	Wand →	Do you like the picture on my *wall*?

Project: Bullying

42	**freak**	Freak, Missgeburt →	Why are you so upset? – Somebody said to me: 'You're a *freak*.'
	get, got, got	werden →	I hope the weather will *get* better soon.

> **Get**
> You **get** lost.   You **get** a present.
> ...   jealous.   ...   a prize.
> ...   wet.   ...   a detention.
> ...   upset.
>
> Things **get** better.
> ...   worse.

	Childline	*(Kindernotruf in Großbritannien)*	
	organize	organisieren, koordinieren, veranstalten	
	plan	planen →	Make a plan for your project. – Yes, I must *plan* it carefully.
	present	präsentieren, vorstellen →	⚠ Die zweite Silbe wird betont (anders als bei 'a present' = Geschenk).

next time	nächstes Mal →	Oh no, we haven't got a map! – Sorry, I'll remember *next time*.

Lerncheck Unit 4

Welche Wörter fehlen?　　　　　bully　drink　phone　visit　work
Benutze dasselbe Wort in beiden Sätzen.

1. I'd like a … . I always … lots of water after PE.
2. You must … harder. You can watch TV when you've finished your … .
3. A girl in our class is a … . But she doesn't … me!
4. This isn't our tutor group's first … to London. We … a museum here every year.
5. Can I use your …, please? I must … my parents now.

Unit 5:　Scotland

46

Scotland	Schottland	
mountain	Berg, Gebirge →	*mountain*
lake	See →	
rain	regnen →	Was it rainy yesterday? – Yes, it *rained* all day.
nature	Natur →	Why doesn't Matt like fields and mountains? – He isn't interested in *nature*.
Ben Nevis	*(höchster Berg Schottlands und Großbritanniens)*	
Nessie	*(angebliches Seeungeheuer im schottischen Loch Ness)*	
Loch Ness	*(See in Schottland)*	
loch	*(das schottische Wort für See)* →	This is a lake in England and a *loch* in Scotland.

lake

Where you find water
pond
river
lake (loch)　　**der** See
sea　　　　　　**die** See, das Meer

Scottish	schottisch →	Lots of people like *Scottish* music. ⚠ Das große 'S' nicht vergessen!
ride, rode, ridden	fahren, reiten	

Ride – drive – go
You **ride** a bike.　　　　A **driver** can **drive** a car.
…　　　　a pony.　　　…　　　　　a bus.
　　　　　　　　　　　…　　　　　a taxi.

You're too young to drive.
But you can **go** by car.
Or you can go by bus or by taxi.

---

route	Strecke, Route →	Let's go this way. It's the quickest *route* to the lake.
Edinburgh	*(Großstadt in Schott-land)*	

47 | **person** | Person → | ⚠ Die erste Silbe wird betont.
bed and breakfast (B & B)	Zimmer mit Frühstück, Frühstückspension	
youth hostel	Jugendherberge →	On our class trip we stayed in a *youth hostel*.
cottage	Hütte, Häuschen, Ferienwohnung →	a *cottage* = a small house. There are lots of pretty *cottages* in the village.

> **Places to stay**
> tent
> youth hostel
> bed and breakfast
> cottage
> holiday flat
> hotel

Language

48 | **guest** | Gast → | How many people are staying in your hotel? – We have 38 *guests* right now.

been	gewesen
come	gekommen
order	bestellen →
made	gemacht, getan
taken	gebracht, genommen
not yet	noch nicht →
done	getan, gemacht
Just a minute, please.	Einen Moment bitte.
Superman	Supermann

Would you like to *order* your meal now?

No, I have*n't* found my earring *yet*.

49 | **lose, lost, lost** | verlieren → | Oh no, I've *lost* my bus ticket!
| **eaten** | gegessen, gefressen → | Where are those hamburgers?
| | | – I've already *eaten* them.

ever	jemals
Have you ever been to Germany?	Bist du schon einmal in Deutschland gewesen?

> **Already – not … yet   Ever – never**
> Have you made   – Yes, I've **already** cooked it.
> the dinner?   No, I have**n't** done that **yet**.
> Have you **ever** made curry? – Yes, I have.
>   No, I've **never** done that.

found	gefunden

Text: A photo of Nessie?

50 | **breathe** | atmen → | It's OK. He's still *breathing*.
| **camera** | Kamera, Fotoapparat |
| **could** | konnte/konnten |

51	couldn't	konnte nicht/konnten nicht →	Why didn't you play in our team? – I *couldn't* find my trainers.
	head	Kopf	
	through	durch →	You can see *through* a window.
	model	Modell, Nachbildung →	Andy makes *models* of boats. That's his hobby.
	remote control	Fernsteuerung, Fernbedienung	

Practice

| 53 | bought | gekauft |

Words

| 55 | sound | Laut, Ton | |
| | spelling | Rechtschreibung → | The word guest is easy to say, but the *spelling* is difficult. |

Lerncheck Unit 5

Welche Wörter fehlen?   breathe   guests   mountains   been   cottages

1. Come to the Lake Hotel and … in the fresh air.
2. You can climb … or swim in the lake.
3. In Scotland tourists can stay in … .
4. Susie hasn't … to Edinburgh.
5. Lots of our … come to stay here every year.

Unit 6: My music

58	heavy metal	Heavy Metal	
	jazz	Jazz →	In our band we don't play *jazz*.
	classical	klassisch →	DJs don't usually play *classical* music.
	that	der/die/das, dem/den (Relativpronomen) →	Here's the CD *that* I bought yesterday.
	totally	total, völlig →	I *totally* love 'Yellow'. = I love 'Yellow' very much.
			⚠ Die erste Silbe wird betont.

> **Great music!**
> I **like** jazz.
> I **enjoy** pop music.
> I **totally love** rock music.
> I**'m crazy about** heavy metal.

	break up	sich trennen, Schluss machen →	So Brad isn't Sue's boyfriend? – No, they've *broken up*.
59	recorder	Blockflöte →	Listen! My sister is playing the *recorder*.
	trumpet	Trompete	
	orchestra	Orchester	
	instrument	Instrument	

> **What's your favourite instrument?**
> drums   trombone
> guitar   trumpet
> recorder

	questionnaire	Fragebogen →	Please answer the questions on this *questionnaire*.
	remind somebody	jemanden erinnern →	This rainy weather *reminds me* of Scotland.
	read music	Noten lesen	
60	unhappy	unglücklich →	happy ←→ *unhappy*
	good-looking	gut aussehend →	Is Katie pretty? – Yes, she's very *good-looking*.
	believe	glauben, denken →	⚠ Die zweite Silbe wird betont.
	split, split, split	sich trennen →	Andy and Alex don't play together now. They *split* last year.
	lyrics	Liedtext	
	shocked	schockiert, erschüttert	
	interview	Interview	
	popular	populär, beliebt	

A pop star is usually good-looking.
… popular.
… cool.
… awesome.
Fans are often unhappy when groups break up.
… shocked …
… angry …
… upset …

	title	Titel, Überschrift →	The *title* of their new song is 'Crazy girl'.
			⚠ Der Anfang wird wie 'ti' in 'time' ausgesprochen.

Project: Profile of a band

62	profile	Porträt, Profil
	cover	Titelseite, Einband, Hülle

Lerncheck Unit 6

Welche Wörter fehlen?   unhappy   popular   lyrics   reminds   good-looking   wall

1. 'Shock' is a very … band this year.
2. The singer of the band is tall and … .
3. Lots of girls have a 'Shock' poster on their … .
4. 'Their singer, Matt, is cute,' Anna says. 'He … me of my boyfriend.'
5. But her brother Peter says, 'Their … are too difficult for me.'
6. Lisa is … because she couldn't get tickets for their concert.

Unit 7: Crazy weather

64	temperature	Temperatur →	⚠ Die erste Silbe wird betont.
	degree	Grad →	
	warm	warm →	It's *warm* today.
			– Yes, the *temperature* is 19 *degrees*.
	snow	Schnee	
	thousands	tausende, viele tausend	
	headline	Schlagzeile →	Read this *headline*.

65	rain	Regen →	The weather was very rainy. = We had lots of *rain*.
	town centre	Stadtzentrum	
	flood	Überschwemmung, Hochwasser →	There are *floods* in the street.
	tornado	Tornado →	A *tornado* is a very bad *storm*.
	coast	Küste →	There are lots of nice beaches on the *coast*.
	wind	Wind	
	destroy	zerstören →	We haven't got a car now, because the tornado *destroyed* it.
	storm	Sturm	

How was the weather?

We had snow.	It was cold.
... rain.	... warm.
... floods.	... hot.
... storms.	... cloudy.
... a tornado.	... sunny.

Language

66	Boscastle	*(Dorf an der Nordwest-küste Cornwalls)*	
	Cornwall	*(Halbinsel und Graf-schaft an der Südwest-spitze Englands)*	
	valley	Tal →	There's a *valley* between two mountains.

In the country

mountain	sea
valley	coast
river	beach
lake	

	witchcraft	Hexerei	
	if	wenn, falls; ob →	*If* there's a storm tonight, we'll stay at home.
67	pilot	Pilot/Pilotin	
	helicopter	Hubschrauber	
	fly, flew, flown	fliegen	
	myself	selbst, ich selbst, mich selbst →	Who made this boat? – I made it *myself*.
	disaster	Katastrophe, Unglück →	A *disaster* is a very bad accident.
	save	retten →	Help! Please *save* me!
	pull	ziehen →	*Pull!*

What can you do with a box?
pull
push
put down
carry
wear

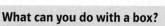

| | themselves | selbst, sie selbst, sich selbst → | Some people talk to *themselves*. |
| | herself | selbst, sie selbst, sich selbst | |

| **It's a pity.** | Es ist schade./Es ist bedauerlich. | |
| **yourself** | selbst, du selbst, dich selbst → | You shouldn't talk about *yourself* all the time. |

> **When something bad happens to somebody, you can say:**
> "What's the matter?"
> "What's wrong?"
> "Are you OK?"
> "It's a pity."

Text: The storm

68	**witch**	Hexe →	a *witch*
	dead	tot	
69	**line**	Seil, Leine →	I hope the *line* doesn't break.
	spoke	sprach/sprachen	

Practice

70	**himself**	selbst, er selbst, sich selbst →	Must we help Luke with his homework? – No, he can do it *himself*.
	ourselves	selbst, wir selbst, uns selbst →	We made all the food for the party *ourselves*.
	speaker	Sprecher →	A *speaker* speaks.
71	**euro**	Euro	
	sign	Schild, Zeichen	

Fire Action – Verhalten bei Feuer (page 71)

operate	betätigen
fire alarm	Feuermelder
building	Gebäude
exit	Ausgang
report to	sich melden
assembly point	Sammelplatz
collect	einsammeln
personal belongings	persönliches Eigentum
re-enter	wieder hineingehen
safe	sicher
in case of	falls
fire	Feuer

Lerncheck Unit 7

Kannst du Mini-Dialoge zusammenstellen? Ein Satz aus A passt zu einem Satz aus B.

A	**B**
What will the weather be like?	I'll stay at home and watch a disaster film.
Yesterday a tornado came to England.	Yes, the water carried it into the sea.
It's a pity about the boat.	Cold, with some rain and storms.
What will you do if it rains?	Yes, I know. Helicopters saved them.
People were on houses and in trees.	That's right. It destroyed campsites at the south coast.

Unit 8: Top sports

76 **chess** Schach → Do you play *chess*? – Yes, I do.

champion Champion, Meister/ Meisterin

prefer vorziehen, bevorzugen

active aktiv → Annie does sports every day. She's very *active*.

karate Karate → We do *karate* at our sports club.

darts Darts → Can you play *darts*?

spectator sport Publikumssport → Thousands of *spectators* watch Formula One, but they don't drive those fast cars. It's a *spectator sport*.

spectator Zuschauer/Zuschaue- rin →

bungee jumping Bungeespringen → Our PE teacher does *bungee jumping*. She goes surfing, too.

77 **extreme sports** Extremsport → *Extreme sports* are exciting, but they are dangerous, too.

extreme extrem; äußerster/ äußerste/äußerstes

So many sports		
You **do** sports.		You **play** darts.
... bungee jumping.		... chess.
... karate.		... basketball.
... PE.		... football.
	You **go** ice skating.	
	... surfing.	
	... swimming.	

newspaper Zeitung

What can you read?	
a book	a newspaper
a comic	a report
a magazine	

78 **type** Typ

couch potato Fernsehglotzer/Fern- sehglotzerin, Couchpo- tato → Switch off that TV! You're a terrible *couch potato*.

once einmal; einst

once a week einmal pro Woche → They do bungee jumping *once a week*, every Saturday afternoon.

How often ...?
once a week
three times a year
five times a day

join   beitreten, sich an-
schließen, verbinden →   I go to the karate club every week. I *joined* it last year.

won   gewann/gewannen

Sports: Who? Where? What?

people	places	events
spectator	changing room	competition
player	sports field	race
team	sports hall	home game
coach	swimming pool	away game
champion		training

What people do
They practise.
…   train.
…   join a club.
…   hit a ball.
…   kick … .
…   throw … .
…   run.
…   jump.
…   win a game.
…   win a prize.

---

congratulations   Glückwunsch

79   **percent (%)**   Prozent

won   gewonnen

Project: Sports clubs

80   **as**   wie →

step   Schritt

As always, you've finished your meal first.

Lerncheck Unit 8

Welche Wörter fehlen?   champions   joined   newspaper   prefer   spectators

1. Hundreds of … are watching the bungee jumping.
2. A man is taking photos for a … .
3. Caroline is new in the chess club. She … it last week.
4. But Frank says, "I think chess is boring. I … basketball."
5. His favourite team often wins. They are the … .

In dieser alphabetischen Liste ist das gesamte Vokabular von *Let's go 3* enthalten. Namen werden in einer gesonderten Liste am Ende des Vokabulars aufgelistet.
Das Zeichen ⟨ ⟩ bei einer Angabe weist darauf hin, dass das Wort zum rezeptiven Wortschatz zählt.
Wendungen, die aus mehreren Wörtern bestehen, werden meist unter mehreren Stichwörtern aufgeführt.
So ist z. B. *at home* unter *at* und *home* zu finden.
Die Zahlen verweisen auf das erstmalige Vorkommen der Wörter, z. B.
act I = Das Wort kam in Band I vor.
ago II = Das Wort kam in Band II vor.
already U4, 38 = Unit 4, Seite 38

A

a [ə] ein/eine I
⟨a bit⟩ [ə'bɪt] ein wenig **U5,** 57
a hundred [ə'hʌndrəd] hundert II
about [ə'baʊt] ungefähr, circa II
about [ə'baʊt] über I; wegen II
accident ['æksɪdnt] Unfall II
act [ækt] spielen *(eine Rolle)* I
active ['æktɪv] aktiv **U8,** 76
activity [æk'tɪvəti] Aktivität, Tätigkeit I
activity centre [æk'tɪvəti 'sentə] Freizeitzentrum I
add [æd] addieren, hinzufügen **U2,** 20
⟨addicted to⟩ [ə'dɪktɪd tʊ] süchtig nach **U2,** 25
address [ə'dres] Adresse II
adventure [əd'ventʃə] Abenteuer II
after ['ɑːftə] nach I
after that ['ɑːftə 'ðæt] danach II
… is after you [ɪz 'ɑːftə 'juː] … verfolgt dich, … ist hinter dir her I
afternoon [ɑːftə'nuːn] Nachmittag II
again [ə'gen] wieder, noch einmal I
against [ə'genst] gegen **U3,** 27
ago [ə'gəʊ] vor II
air [eə] Luft II
airport ['eəpɔːt] Flughafen II
be **alive** [bi: ə'laɪv] am Leben sein, leben II
all [ɔːl] alle, alles I
all evening [ɔːl 'iːvnɪŋ] den ganzen Abend lang I
almost ['ɔːlməʊst] fast, beinahe II
alone [ə'ləʊn] alleine I
Leave me alone. [liːv mi: ə'ləʊn] Lass mich in Ruhe. I
along [ə'lɒŋ] entlang I
alphabet ['ælfəbet] Alphabet I
already [ɔːl'redi] schon, bereits **U4,** 38

also ['ɔːlsəʊ] auch I
always ['ɔːlweɪz] immer I
an [ən] ein/eine I
and [ænd] und I
angry ['æŋgri] zornig, wütend I
animal ['ænɪml] Tier I
anorak ['ænəræk] Anorak II
another [ə'nʌðə] noch einer/eine/eins; ein anderer/eine andere/ein anderes II
answer ['ɑːnsə] Antwort I
answer ['ɑːnsə] beantworten, antworten I
any ['eni] irgendwelche, irgendeiner/irgendeine/irgendein II
not … any ['nɒt 'eni] kein/keine II
anybody ['enibɒdi] irgendjemand, jeder (beliebige) II
anything ['eniθɪŋ] irgendetwas II
Anything else? [eniθɪŋ 'els] Sonst noch etwas? I
not … anything ['nɒt 'eniθɪŋ] nichts II
apple ['æpl] Apfel I
April ['eɪprl] April I
are [ɑː] bist I; sind, seid I
argue ['ɑːgjuː] diskutieren, streiten I
arrive [ə'raɪv] ankommen II
art [ɑːt] Kunst I
as [æz] während, als **U2,** 20
as [æz] wie **U8,** 80
ask [ɑːsk] fragen I
at [æt] in, auf, an, bei I; um I
at home [æt 'həʊm] zu Hause; daheim I
at the weekend [æt ðə wiːk'end] am Wochenende I
attic ['ætɪk] Dachboden, Speicher I
audition [ɔː'dɪʃn] Vorsingen, Vorspielen II
August ['ɔːgəst] August I
autumn ['ɔːtəm] Herbst I
away [ə'weɪ] weg I
away game [ə'weɪ geɪm] Auswärtsspiel **U3,** 33

awesome ['ɔːsəm] beeindruckend, super II
awful ['ɔːfl] furchtbar, scheußlich I

B

back [bæk] zurück I
Text me back. [tekst mi: 'bæk] Schreib zurück (SZ). II
bad [bæd] schlecht, schlimm II
bag [bæg] Tasche I
ball [bɔːl] Ball I
balloon [bə'luːn] Luftballon I
band [bænd] Band, Gruppe I
bark [bɑːk] bellen I
basketball ['bɑːskɪtbɔːl] Basketball I
bathroom ['bɑːθruːm] Badezimmer I
be, was, been [bi:, wɒz, bi:n] sein I
be alive [bi: ə'laɪv] am Leben sein, leben II
be interested in [bɪ 'ɪntrəstɪd ɪn] interessiert sein an, sich interessieren für **U4,** 39
be lucky [bi: 'lʌki] Glück haben I
Be quiet. [bi: 'kwaɪət] Sei/Seid leise. I
be right [bi: 'raɪt] Recht haben II
be scared [bi: 'skeəd] Angst haben, verängstigt sein II
be wrong [bi: 'rɒŋ] Unrecht haben **U2,** 23
Have you ever been to Germany? [hæv ju: evə bi:n tʊ 'dʒɜːməni] Bist du schon einmal in Deutschland gewesen? **U5,** 49
beach [bi:tʃ] Strand I
because [bɪ'kɒz] weil I
bed [bed] Bett I
bed and breakfast (B & B) [bed n 'brekfəst] Zimmer mit Frühstück, Frühstückspension **U5,** 47

go to bed [gəʊ tə 'bed] schlafen gehen, ins Bett gehen **I**
bedroom ['bedruːm] Schlafzimmer **I**
before [bɪ'fɔː] bevor **U3**, 30
behind [bɪ'haɪnd] hinter **I**
believe [bɪ'liːv] glauben, denken **U6**, 60
best [best] der/die/das beste **II**
better ['betə] besser **II**
between [bɪ'twiːn] zwischen **II**
big [bɪg] groß **I**
bike [baɪk] Fahrrad **I**
bill [bɪl] Rechnung **U2**, 20
bird [bɜːd] Vogel **I**
birthday ['bɜːθdeɪ] Geburtstag **I**
Happy birthday! ['hæpi 'bɜːθdeɪ] Herzlichen Glückwunsch zum Geburtstag! **I**
black [blæk] schwarz **II**
blonde [blɒnd] blond **II**
blue [bluː] blau **I**
board [bɔːd] Tafel, Anschlagtafel, schwarzes Brett **I**
boat [bəʊt] Boot, Schiff **I**
book [bʊk] Buch, Heft **I**
book [bʊk] buchen **II**
boring ['bɔːrɪŋ] langweilig **I**
⟨both⟩ [bəʊθ] beide **U3**, 37
box [bɒks] Kiste, Schachtel **I**
boy [bɔɪ] Junge **I**
boy band ['bɔɪ bænd] Boy Group **I**
boyfriend ['bɔɪfrend] Freund **I**
break [breɪk] Pause **II**
break, broke, broken [breɪk, brəʊk, 'brəʊkn] brechen, zerbrechen **U4**, 41
break up [breɪk 'ʌp] sich trennen, Schluss machen **U6**, 58
breakfast ['brekfəst] Frühstück **I**
for breakfast [fə 'brekfəst] zum Frühstück **II**
have breakfast [hæv 'brekfəst] frühstücken **II**
break-in ['breɪkɪn] Einbruch **I**
breathe [briːð] atmen **U5**, 50
breathe in [briːð 'ɪn] einatmen **II**
British ['brɪtɪʃ] britisch **II**
broken ['brəʊkn] kaputt **I**
brother ['brʌðə] Bruder **I**
brown [braʊn] braun **I**
bull [bʊl] Stier, Bulle **I**
bully ['bʊli] tyrannisieren, drangsalieren **U4**, 40
bungee jumping ['bʌndʒi dʒʌmpɪŋ] Bungeespringen **U8**, 76
bus [bʌs] Bus **I**

by (bus) [baɪ 'bʌs] mit (dem Bus) **I**
bush [bʊʃ] Busch, Gebüsch **I**
busy ['bɪzi] beschäftigt **I**
but [bʌt] aber **I**
butter ['bʌtə] Butter **I**
button ['bʌtn] Knopf, Schaltfläche **II**
buy, bought, bought [baɪ, bɔːt, bɔːt] kaufen **I**
by [baɪ] von **I**
⟨by using ...⟩ [baɪ 'juːzɪŋ] indem Sie ... benutzen **U7**, 75
by (bus) [baɪ 'bʌs] mit (dem Bus) **I**

C

café ['kæfeɪ] Café **I**
cafeteria [kæfə'tɪərɪə] Cafeteria **I**
cake [keɪk] Kuchen **I**
call [kɔːl] rufen, anrufen **I**
caller ['kɔːlə] Anrufer/Anruferin **I**
⟨camel⟩ ['kæml] Kamel **U1**, 19
camera ['kæmrə] Kamera, Fotoapparat **U5**, 50
camping trip ['kæmpɪŋ trɪp] Campingausflug, Campingtrip **II**
campsite ['kæmpsaɪt] Campingplatz, Zeltplatz **II**
can [kæn] können **I**
can't [kɑːnt] nicht können **I**
car [kɑː] Auto **I**
car park ['kɑː pɑːk] Parkplatz **I**
card [kɑːd] Karte **I**
card trick ['kɑːd trɪk] Kartentrick **I**
careful ['keəfl] vorsichtig, sorgfältig **I**
caretaker ['keəteɪkə] Hausmeister/Hausmeisterin **I**
carnival ['kɑːnɪvl] Karneval, Volksfest **U1**, 8
carrot ['kærət] Karotte **II**
carry ['kæri] tragen **I**
cartoon [kɑː'tuːn] Cartoon, Zeichentrickfilm **I**
castle ['kɑːsl] Schloss **II**
cat [kæt] Katze **I**
CCTV [siːsiːtiː'viː] Videoüberwachungsanlage **II**
CD [siː'diː] CD **I**
chair [tʃeə] Stuhl **I**
champion ['tʃæmpiən] Champion, Meister/Meisterin **U8**, 77

change to ['tʃeɪndʒ tʊ] umsteigen nach **U1**, 12
changing room ['tʃeɪndʒɪŋ ruːm] Umkleideraum **II**
chatterbox ['tʃætəbɒks] Plappermaul **I**
cheap [tʃiːp] billig **II**
check [tʃek] prüfen, kontrollieren **II**
checklist ['tʃeklɪst] Checkliste, Kontrollliste **II**
cheese [tʃiːz] Käse **I**
chess [tʃes] Schach **U8**, 76
chicken ['tʃɪkɪn] Huhn, Hähnchen **II**
children (pl.) ['tʃɪldrn] Kinder **I**
Chinese [tʃaɪ'niːz] chinesisch **II**
chips [tʃɪps] Pommes frites **II**
chocolate ['tʃɒklət] Schokolade **I**
church [tʃɜːtʃ] Kirche **I**
cinema ['sɪnəmə] Kino **I**
city ['sɪti] Stadt, Großstadt **II**
class [klɑːs] Schulklasse, Klasse **U1**, 9
classical ['klæsikl] klassisch **U6**, 58
classroom ['klɑːsruːm] Klassenzimmer **II**
clever ['klevə] klug **I**
click [klɪk] klicken **U2**, 20
click on [klɪk 'ɒn] anklicken **II**
climb [klaɪm] klettern **I**
clock [klɒk] Uhr **I**
... o'clock [ə'klɒk] ... Uhr **I**
close [kləʊz] schließen **I**
⟨close⟩ [kləʊs] nahe **U3**, 37
closed [kləʊzd] geschlossen **U1**, 15
clothes [kləʊðz] Kleider, Kleidung **I**
cloudy ['klaʊdi] bewölkt, wolkig **I**
clown [klaʊn] Clown **I**
club [klʌb] Club, Verein **II**
coach [kəʊtʃ] Trainer **U3**, 28
coal mine ['kəʊl maɪn] Kohlenbergwerk, Kohlengrube **U3**, 27
coast [kəʊst] Küste **U7**, 65
coffee ['kɒfi] Kaffee **I**
have a coffee [hæv ə 'kɒfi] Kaffee trinken **I**
cold [kəʊld] kalt **I**
colour ['kʌlə] Farbe **II**
What colour is ...? [wɒt 'kʌlər ɪz] Welche Farbe hat ...? **I**
come, came, come [kʌm, keɪm, kam] kommen **I**
came out: I came out [keɪm 'aʊt] ich kam heraus/ich bin herausgekommen **II**

come from ['kʌm frɒm] kommen aus **II**

Come on! [kʌm 'ɒn] Komm!/ Kommt! **I**

comic ['kɒmɪk] Comicheft **I**

communication [kəmjʊːnɪ'keɪʃn] Kommunikation **U2**, 24

competition [kɒmpə'tɪʃn] Wettbewerb, Wettkampf, Turnier **I**

computer [kəm'pjuːtə] Computer **I**

concert ['kɒnsət] Konzert **U3**, 28

congratulations [kəngrætʃʊ'leɪʃnz] Glückwunsch **U8**, 78

⟨**contain**⟩ [kən'teɪn] enthalten **U1**, 19

cook [kʊk] kochen **II**

cool [kuːl] prima, cool **I**

cornflakes ['kɔːnfleɪks] Cornflakes **I**

cost, cost, cost [kɒst, kɒst, kɒst] kosten **II**

cottage ['kɒtɪdʒ] Hütte, Häuschen, Ferienwohnung **U5**, 47

couch potato [kaʊtʃ pə'teɪtəʊ] Fernsehglotzer/Fernsehglotzerin, Couchpotato **U8**, 78

could [kʊd] könnte/könnten **II**; konnte/konnten **U5**, 50

couldn't ['kʊdnt] konnte nicht/konnten nicht **U5**, 51

⟨**counter**⟩ ['kaʊntə] Theke **U5**, 57

country ['kʌntri] Land **II**

cousin ['kʌzn] Cousin/Cousine, Vetter **I**

cover ['kʌvə] Titelseite, Einband, Hülle **U6**, 62

cow [kaʊ] Kuh **I**

crazy ['kreɪzi] verrückt **I**

credit ['kredɪt] Guthaben, Kredit **U1**, 13

cricket ['krɪkɪt] Kricket **I**

criminal ['krɪmɪnl] Verbrecher/Verbrecherin **I**

cup [kʌp] Tasse **II**

cupboard ['kʌbəd] Küchenschrank, Schrank **I**

curry ['kʌri] Curry, Currygericht **II**

⟨**cut, cut, cut**⟩ [kʌt, kʌt, kʌt] schneiden **U5**, 57

cute [kjuːt] süß **II**

D

dad [dæd] Papa **I**

dance [dɑːns] tanzen **I**

dancer ['dɑːnsə] Tänzer/Tänzerin **II**

dangerous ['deɪndʒrəs] gefährlich **I**

dark [dɑːk] dunkel **II**

darts [dɑːts] Darts **U8**, 76

daughter ['dɔːtə] Tochter **II**

day [deɪ] Tag **I**

dead [ded] tot **U7**, 68

Dear [dɪə] Lieber/Liebe/Liebes *(in Briefanrede)* **I**

December [dɪ'sembə] Dezember **I**

decide [dɪ'saɪd] entscheiden **II**

degree [dɪ'griː] Grad **U7**, 64

demonstration [demən'streɪʃn] Demonstration **U1**, 13

departure [dɪ'pɑːtʃə] Abflug, Abreise **II**

⟨**desert**⟩ ['dezət] Wüste **U1**, 19

design [dɪ'zaɪn] Muster, Entwurf **I**

destroy [dɪ'strɔɪ] zerstören **U7**, 65

detective [dɪ'tektɪv] Kriminalbeamter/Kriminalbeamtin, Detektiv/Detektivin **II**

detective story [dɪ'tektɪv 'stɔːri] Kriminalroman, Detektivgeschichte **II**

detention [dɪ'tentʃn] Nachsitzen, Haft **U4**, 40

⟨**detergent**⟩ [dɪ'tɜːdʒnt] Waschmittel **U7**, 75

dialogue ['daɪəlɒg] Dialog, Gespräch **U1**, 8

die [daɪ] sterben **II**

dictionary ['dɪkʃnri] Wörterbuch **U1**, 16

diet ['daɪət] Diät, Nahrung **II**

different ['dɪfrnt] verschieden, anders **I**

difficult ['dɪfɪklt] schwierig **II**

dining room ['daɪnɪŋ ruːm] Esszimmer **I**

dinner ['dɪnə] Abendessen **I**

have dinner [hæv 'dɪnə] zu Abend essen **I**

disaster [dɪ'zɑːstə] Katastrophe, Unglück **U7**, 67

disco ['dɪskəʊ] Disko **I**

discus ['dɪskəs] Diskus **I**

DJ [di: 'dʒeɪ] Diskjockey **I**

do, did, done [duː, dɪd, dʌn] tun, machen **I**

do sports [duː 'spɔːts] Sport (-arten) treiben **I**

dog [dɒg] Hund **I**

dog-tired [dɒg'taɪəd] hundemüde **I**

⟨**dollar ($)**⟩ ['dɒlə] Dollar *(amerikanische Währungseinheit)* **U2**, 25

door [dɔː] Tür **I**

⟨**doughnut**⟩ ['dəʊnʌt] Donut **U5**, 57

down [daʊn] herunter, hinunter, nach unten **II**

download [daʊn'ləʊd] herunterladen **I**

draw, drew, drawn [drɔː, druː, drɔːn] zeichnen **I**

dress [dres] Kleid **II**

drink [drɪŋk] Getränk **I**

drink, drank, drunk [drɪŋk, dræŋk, drʌŋk] trinken **I**

drive, drove, driven [draɪv, drəʊv, 'drɪvn] fahren **I**

driver ['draɪvə] Fahrer/Fahrerin **I**

drums [drʌmz] Schlagzeug **I**

duck [dʌk] Ente **I**

⟨**dummy**⟩ ['dʌmi] Dummkopf **U5**, 57

dungeon ['dʌndʒən] Verlies, Kerker **II**

during ['djʊərɪŋ] während **U1**, 8

DVD [diːviːˈdiː] DVD **I**

DVD player [diːviːˈdiː pleɪə] DVD-Spieler **I**

E

earring ['ɪərɪŋ] Ohrring **II**

east [iːst] Osten **I**

easy ['iːzi] einfach **I**

eat, ate, eaten [iːt, et/eɪt, 'iːtn] essen, fressen **I**

egg [eg] Ei **I**

eleven [ɪ'levn] elf **I**

Anything **else?** [eniθɪŋ 'els] Sonst noch etwas? **I**

e-mail ['iːmeɪl] E-Mail **I**

embarrassing [ɪm'bærəsɪŋ] peinlich, unangenehm **II**

more embarrassing [mɔː ɪm'bærəsɪŋ] peinlicher, unangenehmer **II**

the most embarrassing [ðə məʊst ɪm'bærəsɪŋ] der/die/das peinlichste, der/die/das unangenehmste **II**

end [end] Ende, Schluss **I**

ending ['endɪŋ] Ende, Schluss **U2**, 23

English ['ɪŋglɪʃ] Engländer/Engländerin **I**; Englisch **II** in English [ɪn 'ɪŋglɪʃ] auf Englisch **U2**, 24

enjoy [ɪn'dʒɔɪ] mögen, genießen **II**

⟨**enter**⟩ ['entə] betreten **U5**, 57

⟨environment⟩ [ɪnˈvaɪərnmənt] Umwelt **U7**, 75
euro [ˈjʊərəʊ] Euro **U7**, 71
evening [ˈiːvnɪŋ] Abend **I**
all evening [ɔːl ˈiːvnɪŋ] den ganzen Abend lang **I**
in the evening [ɪn ðiː ˈiːvnɪŋ] am Abend; abends **I**
event [ɪˈvent] Ereignis, Veranstaltung **I**
ever [ˈevə] jemals **U5**, 49
Have you ever been to Germany? [hæv ju: evə biːn tʊ ˈdʒɜːməni] Bist du schon einmal in Deutschland gewesen? **U5**, 49
every [ˈevri] jeder/jede/jedes **I**
everybody [ˈevribɒdi] jeder **I**
exchange [ɪksˈtʃeɪndʒ] Austausch **I**
exchange [ɪksˈtʃeɪndʒ] tauschen, wechseln **II**
excited [ɪkˈsaɪtɪd] aufgeregt, begeistert **U1**, 9
exciting [ɪkˈsaɪtɪŋ] spannend, aufregend **II**
Excuse me. [ɪkˈskjuːz mi] Entschuldigung. **I**
exercise [ˈeksəsaɪz] Übung **II**
exercise book [ˈeksəsaɪz bʊk] Übungsheft **I**
exhibition [eksɪˈbɪʃn] Ausstellung **II**
expensive [ɪkˈspensɪv] teuer **I**
extra [ˈekstrə] zusätzlich; Zusatz **U4**, 40
extreme [ɪkˈstriːm] extrem; äußerster/äußerste/äußerstes **U8**, 76
extreme sports [ɪkˈstriːm spɔːts] Extremsport **U8**, 76
eye [aɪ] Auge **II**
⟨eye level⟩ [ˈaɪ levl] Augenhöhe **U3**, 37
⟨eyehole⟩ [ˈaɪhəʊl] Augenloch **U5**, 57
⟨eyelash⟩ [ˈaɪlæʃ] Wimper **U1**, 19

F

face [feɪs] Gesicht **I**
face painting [ˈfeɪs peɪntɪŋ] Kinderschminken **I**
fair [feə] Jahrmarkt, Schulfest **I**
fair [feə] fair, gerecht **II**
fall, fell, fallen [fɔːl, fel, ˈfɔːln] fallen **II**
family [ˈfæmli] Familie **I**

famous [ˈfeɪməs] berühmt **I**
fan [fæn] Fan **I**
fancy [ˈfænsi] mögen **II**
fantastic [fænˈtæstik] fantastisch, toll **I**
farm [fɑːm] Bauernhof **I**
farm machine [ˈfɑːm məʃiːn] landwirtschaftliche Maschine **I**
fast [fɑːst] schnell **II**
⟨fat⟩ [fæt] Fett **U1**, 19
father [ˈfɑːðə] Vater **I**
favourite [ˈfeɪvrɪt] Lieblings- **I**
February [ˈfebruri] Februar **I**
feed, fed, fed [fiːd, fed, fed] füttern **I**
feel, felt, felt [fiːl, felt, felt] fühlen, sich fühlen **U3**, 30
⟨feet⟩ [fiːt] Füße **U1**, 19
felt-tip [felt'tɪp] Filzstift **I**
festival [ˈfestɪvl] Fest **I**
fetch [fetʃ] abholen, holen **I**
field [fiːld] Acker, Feld **I**
fight, fought, fought [faɪt, fɔːt, fɔːt] kämpfen, sich prügeln **I**
film [fɪlm] Film **I**
final [ˈfaɪnl] Finale **II**
find, found, found [faɪnd, faʊnd, faʊnd] finden **I**
find out [faɪnd ˈaʊt] herausfinden **I**
find out about [faɪnd ˈaʊt əˈbaʊt] lernen über, erfahren über **II**
fine [faɪn] in Ordnung **I**
Fine, thanks. [ˈfaɪn θæŋks] Danke, gut. **I**
⟨finger⟩ [ˈfɪŋgə] Finger **U3**, 37
finish [ˈfɪnɪʃ] beenden **I**; enden, aufhören **II**
fire engine [ˈfaɪə endʒɪn] Feuerwehrauto **I**
first [fɜːst] zuerst **II**
fish pl. **fish** [fɪʃ] Fisch **I**
fit [fɪt] fit, in Form **II**
flat [flæt] Wohnung **I**
flight [flaɪt] Flug **II**
flight number [flaɪt ˈnʌmbə] Flugnummer **II**
flood [flʌd] Überschwemmung, Hochwasser **U7**, 65
fly, flew, flown [flaɪ, fluː, fləʊn] fliegen **U7**, 67
⟨focus⟩ [ˈfəʊkəs] konzentriert blicken, fokussieren **U3**, 37
follow [ˈfɒləʊ] folgen **I**
food [fuːd] Nahrung, Essen **I**
football [ˈfʊtbɔːl] Fußball **I**
for [fɔː] für **I**
for ... years [fɔː ˈjɪəz] ... Jahre lang **U1**, 8

forget, forgot, forgotten [fəˈget, fəˈgɒt, fəˈgɒtn] vergessen **U3**, 28
fork [fɔːk] Gabel **II**
form [fɔːm] Vordruck **II**
freak [friːk] Freak, Missgeburt **U4**, 42
free [friː] kostenlos, frei **U1**, 10
fresh [freʃ] frisch **I**
Friday [ˈfraɪdeɪ] Freitag **I**
friend [frend] Freund/Freundin **I**
frog [frɒg] Frosch **I**
from [frɒm] aus, von **I**
from ... to [frɒm tʊ] von ... bis **I**
I'm from ... . [ˈaɪm frɒm] Ich komme aus ... . **I**
Where are you from? [weər ɑː jə ˈfrɒm] Woher kommst du? **I**
at the **front** [æt ðə ˈfrʌnt] vorne **U1**, 15
fruit [fruːt] Obst, Frucht **II**
Have **fun!** [həv ˈfʌn] Viel Spaß! **II**
is/are fun [fʌn] macht/machen Spaß **I**
funny [ˈfʌni] komisch, lustig **I**
future [ˈfjuːtʃə] Zukunft **U2**, 24

G

galaxy [ˈgæləksi] Galaxie **I**
game [geɪm] Spiel **I**
garden [ˈgɑːdn] Garten **I**
gate [geɪt] Tor, Flugsteig **II**
Geography [dʒiˈɒgrəfi] Erdkunde, Geografie **II**
German [ˈdʒɜːmən] Deutsch **I**; deutsch; Deutscher/Deutsche **U1**, 14
get, got, got [get, gɒt, gɒt] bekommen, kriegen **I**; kaufen **II**; werden **U4**, 42
get lost [get ˈlɒst] sich verlaufen **I**
get off [get ˈɒf] aussteigen **U1**, 12
get up [get ˈʌp] aufstehen **I**
ghost [gəʊst] Geist **II**
girl [gɜːl] Mädchen **I**
girlfriend [ˈgɜːlfrend] Freundin **II**
give, gave, given [gɪv, geɪv, ˈgɪvn] geben, schenken **I**
Just give it to me. [dʒʌst ˈgɪv ɪt tʊ miː] Jetzt aber her damit. **II**
glass [glɑːs] Glas **I**

glasses [ˈglɑːsɪz] Brille **I**
go, **went**, **gone** [gəʊ, went, gɒn] gehen, fahren **I**
go ice skating [gəʊ ˈaɪs skeɪtɪŋ] schlittschuhlaufen gehen **II**
go jogging [gəʊ ˈdʒɒgɪŋ] joggen gehen **I**
go on [gəʊ ˈɒn] weitermachen, weitergehen **I**
go on a trip [gəʊ ɒn ə ˈtrɪp] einen Ausflug machen, eine Reise machen **II**
go out [gəʊ ˈaʊt] ausgehen, ausfahren **I**
go rowing [gəʊ ˈrəʊɪŋ] rudern gehen **II**
go shopping [gəʊ ˈʃɒpɪŋ] einkaufen gehen **II**
go surfing [gəʊ ˈsɜːfɪŋ] surfen gehen **II**
go swimming [gəʊ ˈswɪmɪŋ] schwimmen gehen **I**
go to bed [gəʊ tə ˈbed] schlafen gehen, ins Bett gehen **I**
go together [gəʊ ˈtəgeðə] zusammenpassen **U1**, 17
go with [gəʊ ˈwɪð] zusammenpassen mit **II**
going to [ˈgəʊɪŋ tʊ] vorhaben, werden **II**
golf [gɒlf] Golf **I**
good [gʊd] gut **I**
good-looking [gʊd ˈlʊkɪŋ] gut aussehend **U6**, 60
good at [ˈgʊd æt] gut in **I**
Good morning. [gʊd ˈmɔːnɪŋ] Guten Morgen. **I**
Goodbye. [gʊdˈbaɪ] Auf Wiedersehen. **I**
grade [greɪd] Note **II**
grandad [ˈgrændæd] Opa **U3**, 29
grandma [ˈgrænmɑː] Oma **I**
⟨**grateful**⟩ [ˈgreɪtfl] dankbar **U7**, 75
great [greɪt] großartig **I**
green [griːn] grün **I**
greeting [ˈgriːtɪŋ] Gruß **U3**, 31
group [gruːp] Gruppe **I**
guest [gest] Gast **U5**, 48
guinea pig [ˈgɪni pɪg] Meerschweinchen **I**
guitar [gɪˈtɑː] Gitarre **I**

H

hair [heə] Haar, Haare **II**
half past [hɑːf ˈpɑːst] halb **I**
⟨**half**⟩ [hɑːf] Hälfte; halbe, halber, halbes **U2**, 25

hamburger [ˈhæmbɜːgə] Hamburger **I**
hand [hænd] Hand **II**
happen [ˈhæpn] passieren, geschehen **II**
What's happening? [wɒts ˈhæpenɪŋ] Was geht hier vor? **I**
happy [ˈhæpi] glücklich, froh **I**
Happy birthday! [ˈhæpi ˈbɜːθdeɪ] Herzlichen Glückwunsch zum Geburtstag! **I**
hard [hɑːd] schwierig, hart **I**
hat [hæt] Hut **I**
hate [heɪt] nicht mögen, hassen **I**
have, had, had [hæv, hæd, hæd] haben **II**
have a coffee [hæv ə ˈkɒfi] Kaffee trinken **I**
have breakfast [hæv ˈbrekfəst] frühstücken **I**
have dinner [hæv ˈdɪnə] zu Abend essen **I**
Have fun! [həv ˈfʌn] Viel Spaß! **II**
have got [hæv ˈgɒt] haben, besitzen **I**
have lunch [hæv ˈlʌntʃ] zu Mittag essen **I**
have to [ˈhæv tʊ] müssen **II**
Have you ever been to Germany? [hæv ju: evə biːn tʊ ˈdʒɜːməni] Bist du schon einmal in Deutschland gewesen? **U5**, 49
he [hiː] er **I**
head [hed] Kopf **U5**, 51
headline [ˈhedlaɪn] Schlagzeile **U7**, 64
headteacher [hedˈtiːtʃə] Rektor/Rektorin, Schulleiter/Schulleiterin **U4**, 40
hear, heard, heard [hɪə, hɜːd, hɜːd] hören **I**
heavy metal [hevi ˈmetl] Heavy Metal **U6**, 58
helicopter [ˈhelɪkɒptə] Hubschrauber **U7**, 67
Hello. [helˈəʊ] Hallo. **I**
say hello [seɪ heˈləʊ] Grüße ausrichten **II**
⟨**help**⟩ [help] Hilfe **U7**, 75
help [help] helfen **I**
hen [hen] Henne, Huhn **I**
her [hɜː] ihr/ihre **I**; ihr; sie **I**
here [hɪə] hier **I**
Here you are. [hɪə ju: ˈɑː] Hier bitte. **I**
herself [həˈself] selbst, sie selbst, sich selbst **U7**, 67

Hey! [heɪ] He! **II**
Hi. [haɪ] Hallo. **I**
high [haɪ] hoch **II**
him [hɪm] ihm; ihn **I**
himself [hɪmˈself] selbst, er selbst, sich selbst **U7**, 70
Hindu [ˈhɪnduː] hinduistisch; Hindu **U1**, 9
his [hɪz] sein/seine **I**
history [ˈhɪstri] Geschichte **U2**, 24
hit [hɪt] Hit **II**
hobby [ˈhɒbi] Hobby **I**
hockey [ˈhɒki] Hockey **I**
⟨**hold, held, held**⟩ [həʊld, held, held] halten **U3**, 37
⟨**hole**⟩ [həʊl] Loch **U3**, 37
holiday [ˈhɒlədeɪ] Ferien, Urlaub **I**
home [həʊm] nach Hause **I**; Heim, Zuhause **I**
home game [ˈhəʊm geɪm] Heimspiel **U3**, 33
at home [æt ˈhəʊm] zu Hause; daheim **I**
homework [ˈhəʊmwɜːk] Hausaufgaben **I**
hope [həʊp] hoffen **I**
hot [hɒt] heiß **I**
hotel [həʊˈtel] Hotel **I**
hour [ˈaʊə] Stunde **II**
house [haʊs] Haus **I**
how [haʊ] wie **I**
How are you? [haʊ ˈɑː juː] Wie geht's? **I**
how many [haʊ ˈmeni] wie viele **II**
how much [haʊ ˈmʌtʃ] wie viel **II**
How much are they? [haʊ ˈmʌtʃ ɑː ðeɪ] Wie viel kosten sie? **I**
How much is it? [haʊ ˈmʌtʃ ɪz it] Wie viel kostet es? **I**
How old are you? [haʊ ˈəʊld ɑː juː] Wie alt bist du? **I**
⟨**hump**⟩ [hʌmp] Höcker **U1**, 19
hundreds [ˈhʌndrədz] hunderte, viele hundert **U1**, 8
hungry [ˈhʌŋgri] hungrig **II**
hurt, hurt, hurt [hɜːt, hɜːt, hɜːt] wehtun, schmerzen **II**

I

I [aɪ] ich **I**
I'd like to …. [aɪd ˈlaɪk tʊ] Ich würde gerne …., Ich möchte …. **I**
I'm …. [aɪm] Ich bin …. **I**

I'm from … . ['aɪm frɒm] Ich komme aus … . I
I'm sorry. [aɪm 'sɒri] Tut mir Leid. I
ice cream ['aɪs kri:m] Eis, Eiscreme I
go **ice skating** [gəʊ 'aɪs skeɪtɪŋ] schlittschuhlaufen gehen II
idea [aɪ'dɪə] Idee I
ideal [aɪ'dɪəl] ideal II
if [ɪf] wenn, falls; ob **U7**, 66
ill [ɪl] krank II
important [ɪm'pɔ:tnt] wichtig II
in [ɪn] in, im I
in English [ɪn 'ɪŋglɪʃ] auf Englisch **U2**, 24
in front of [ɪn 'frʌnt əf] vor I
in the evening [ɪn ði: 'i:vnɪŋ] am Abend; abends I
in the morning [ɪn ðə 'mɔ:nɪŋ] am Morgen; morgens I
in there [ɪn 'ðeə] da drin, dort drin I
in town [ɪn 'taʊn] in der Stadt I
⟨index finger⟩ ['ɪndeks fɪŋgə] Zeigefinger **U3**, 37
Indian ['ɪndiən] indisch II
information [ɪnfə'meɪʃn] Information I
Information Centre [ɪnfə'meɪʃn sentə] Informationszentrum I
in-line skates ['ɪnlaɪn skeɪts] Inline-Skates, Inliner I
instrument ['ɪnstrəmənt] Instrument **U6**, 59
be **interested** in [bɪ 'ɪntrəstɪd ɪn] interessiert sein an, sich interessieren für **U4**, 39
interesting ['ɪntrəstɪŋ] interessant I
internet ['ɪntənet] Internet II
on the internet [ɒn ði 'ɪntənet] im Internet II
interview ['ɪntəvju:] Interview **U6**, 60
into ['ɪntə] in, hinein I
invitation [ɪnvɪ'teɪʃn] Einladung II
is [ɪz] ist I
How much is it? [haʊ 'mʌtʃ ɪz ɪt] Wie viel kostet es? I
… is after you [ɪz 'ɑ:ftə 'ju:] … verfolgt dich, … ist hinter dir her I
Is that you? [ɪz ðæt 'ju:] Bist du es? **U2**, 20
it [ɪt] es I
It's … . [ɪts] Es kostet … . I

It's a pity [ɪts ə 'pɪti] Es ist schade./Es ist bedauerlich. **U7**, 67
It's Barbara. [ɪts 'bɑ:brə] Hier ist Barbara. **U2**, 20
It's me. [ɪts 'mi:] Ich bin's. **U2**, 20

J

January ['dʒænjʊri] Januar I
jazz [dʒæz] Jazz **U6**, 58
jealous ['dʒeləs] eifersüchtig II
jeans [dʒi:nz] Jeans II
jigsaw puzzle ['dʒɪgsɔ: pʌzl] Puzzle I
job [dʒɒb] Arbeit, Beruf I; Aufgabe II
go **jogging** [gəʊ 'dʒɒgɪŋ] joggen gehen I
join [dʒɔɪn] beitreten, sich anschließen, verbinden **U8**, 78
joke [dʒəʊk] Witz I
journalist ['dʒɜ:nlɪst] Journalist/Journalistin I
July [dʒʊ'laɪ] Juli I
jump [dʒʌmp] springen II
June [dʒu:n] Juni I
just [dʒʌst] nur II; gerade, soeben II
Just a minute, please. [dʒʌst ə 'mɪnɪt pli:s] Einen Moment bitte. **U5**, 48
Just give it to me. [dʒʌst 'gɪv ɪt tʊ mi:] Jetzt aber her damit. II

K

karaoke [kæri'əʊki] Karaoke I
karate [kə'rɑ:ti] Karate **U8**, 76
kebab [kɪ'bæb] Kebab II
kick [kɪk] schießen, treten II
kilometre [kɪ'lɒmɪtə] Kilometer II
king [kɪŋ] König **U1**, 8
kitchen ['kɪtʃɪn] Küche I
knife pl. **knives** [naɪf] Messer I
know, knew, known [nəʊ, nju:, nəʊn] kennen, wissen I
know about [nəʊ ə'baʊt] wissen von II

L

lake [leɪk] See **U5**, 46
land [lænd] landen II
language ['læŋgwɪdʒ] Sprache **U3**, 26

lantern ['læntən] Laterne I
laptop ['læptɒp] Laptop II
large [lɑ:dʒ] groß, riesig I
last [lɑ:st] letzter/letzte/letztes II
last night [lɑ:st 'naɪt] gestern Abend, gestern Nacht **U3**, 28
late [leɪt] spät, zu spät **U1**, 11
Speak to you later. [spi:k tə jə 'leɪtə] Bis später. **U2**, 21
laugh [lɑ:f] lachen II
lazy ['leɪzi] faul I
learn [lɜ:n] lernen II
leave, left, left [li:v, left, left] verlassen, lassen I; abfliegen II
Leave me alone. [li:v mi: ə'ləʊn] Lass mich in Ruhe. I
left [left] links I
on the left [ɒn ðə 'left] links I
leg [leg] Bein II
lego ['legəʊ] Lego I
leisure centre ['leʒə sentə] Freizeitzentrum II
lesson ['lesn] Unterrichtsstunde, Schulstunde II
let's [lets] lass/lasst uns I
letter ['letə] Buchstabe I; Brief II
library ['laɪbrəri] Bücherei, Bibliothek I
like [laɪk] mögen, gern haben I
I'd like to … . [aɪd 'laɪk tʊ] Ich würde gerne … ., Ich möchte … . I
Would you like … ? [wʊd jə 'laɪk] Möchtest du … ?/ Möchten Sie … ? I
like [laɪk] wie II
What's … like? ['wɒts 'laɪk] Wie ist …? II
line [laɪn] Linie, Zeile **U1**, 12; Seil, Leine **U7**, 69
link [lɪŋk] Verbindung, Link II
list [lɪst] Liste **U1**, 9
listen ['lɪsn] zuhören, anhören I
listen to ['lɪsn tʊ] hören, anhören I
live [lɪv] wohnen, leben I
I lived [lɪvd] ich wohnte/ich habe gewohnt II
living room ['lɪvɪŋ ru:m] Wohnzimmer I
loch [lɒk] (das schottische Wort für See) **U5**, 46
long [lɒŋ] lang I
long jump ['lɒŋ dʒʌmp] Weitsprung I
look [lʊk] sehen, schauen I
good-looking [gʊd 'lʊkɪŋ] gut aussehend **U6**, 60

I've looked at [lʊkt] ich habe angeschaut, ich habe angesehen **II**
look at ['lʊk æt] anschauen, ansehen **I**
look for ['lʊk fɔ:] suchen **I**
lose, lost, lost [lu:z, lɒst, lɒst] verlieren **U5,** 49
lots of ['lɒts əv] viele **I**
loud [laʊd] laut **II**
loudly ['laʊdli] laut **II**
love [lʌv] Liebe **II**
love [lʌv] lieben, gern mögen **I**
be **lucky** [bi: 'lʌki] Glück haben **I**
lunch [lʌntʃ] Mittagessen **I**
have lunch [hæv 'lʌntʃ] zu Mittag essen **I**
lunch break ['lʌntʃ breɪk] Mittagspause **I**
lyrics ['lɪrɪks] Liedtext **U6,** 60

M

magazine [mægə'zi:n] Zeitschrift, Magazin **U1,** 17
make, made, made [meɪk, meɪd, meɪd] machen, tun **I**
make up [meɪk 'ʌp] erfinden, sich ausdenken **I**
man pl. **men** [mæn; men] Mann **I**
many ['meni] viele **II**
how many [haʊ 'meni] wie viele **II**
map [mæp] Stadtplan, Landkarte **I**
March [mɑːtʃ] März **I**
market ['mɑːkɪt] Markt **I**
marry ['mæri] heiraten **II**
match [mætʃ] zuordnen **U1,** 15
matchstick man ['mætʃstɪk mæn] Strichmännchen **I**
Maths [mæθs] Mathematik **II**
What's the **matter?** [wɒts ðe 'mætə] Was ist los? **II**
may [meɪ] dürfen, können **U1,** 13
May [meɪ] Mai **I**
maybe ['meɪbi] vielleicht **I**
me [mi:] mir; mich **I**; ich **II**
It's me. [ɪts 'mi:] Ich bin's. **U2,** 20
meal [mi:l] Mahlzeit, Essen **I**
mean, meant, meant [mi:n, ment, ment] bedeuten, heißen **I**
meat [mi:t] Fleisch **II**
mediation [mi:dɪ'eɪʃn] Sprachmittlung **U1,** 15

meet, met, met [mi:t, met, met] treffen, sich treffen, kennen lernen **I**
Nice to meet you. [naɪs tʊ 'mi:t ju:] Schön dich kennen zu lernen. **I**
meeting place ['mi:tɪŋ pleɪs] Treffpunkt **I**
message ['mesɪdʒ] Mitteilung, Nachricht **II**
metre ['mi:tə] Meter **II**
mice [maɪs] Mäuse **II**
⟨**middle**⟩ ['mɪdl] Mitte **U3,** 37
milk [mɪlk] Milch **I**
million ['mɪljən] Million **II**
mine [maɪn] Mine **U3,** 29
miner ['maɪnə] Bergarbeiter/Bergarbeiterin **U3,** 29
minute [mɪ'nɪt] Minute **U2,** 20
Just a minute, please. [dʒʌst ə 'mɪnɪt pli:s] Einen Moment bitte. **U5,** 48
miss [mɪs] vermissen, verpassen, verfehlen **U1,** 10
mobile ['məʊbaɪl] Handy **U2,** 20
mobile phone [məʊbaɪl 'fəʊn] Handy, Mobiltelefon **I**
model ['mɒdl] Modell, Nachbildung **U5,** 51
modern ['mɒdn] modern **I**
Monday ['mʌndeɪ] Montag **I**
money ['mʌni] Geld **I**
monster ['mɒnstə] Monster, Ungeheuer **I**
month [mʌnθ] Monat **I**
more [mɔː] mehr **II**
more embarrassing [mɔː ɪm'bærəsɪŋ] peinlicher, unangenehmer **II**
morning ['mɔːnɪŋ] Morgen, Vormittag **I**
in the morning [ɪn ðe 'mɔːnɪŋ] am Morgen; morgens **I**
the next morning [ðə nekst 'mɔːnɪŋ] am nächsten Morgen **U3,** 31
mother ['mʌðə] Mutter **I**
mountain ['maʊntɪn] Berg, Gebirge **U5,** 46
mouse [maʊs] Maus **I**
MP3 player [empi:'θri: pleɪə] MP3 Player **II**
Mr ['mɪstə] (Anrede) Herr **I**
Mrs ['mɪsɪz] (Anrede) Frau **I**
much [mʌtʃ] viel **I**
how much [haʊ 'mʌtʃ] wie viel **II**
How much are they? [haʊ 'mʌtʃ ɑ: ðeɪ] Wie viel kosten sie? **I**

How much is it? [haʊ 'mʌtʃ ɪz it] Wie viel kostet es? **I**
mum [mʌm] Mama **I**
museum [mjuː'zi:əm] Museum **II**
music ['mjuːzɪk] Musik **I**
read music [ri:d 'mjuːzɪk] Noten lesen **U6,** 59
must [mʌst] müssen **I**
mustn't ['mʌsnt] nicht dürfen **II**
my [maɪ] mein/meine **I**
My name is …. [maɪ 'neɪm ɪz] Ich heiße …. **I**
myself [maɪ'self] selbst, ich selbst, mich selbst **U7,** 67

N

name [neɪm] Name **I**
My name is …. [maɪ 'neɪm ɪz] Ich heiße …. **I**
What's your name? [wɒts jɔː 'neɪm] Wie heißt du? **I**
⟨**nation**⟩ ['neɪʃn] Land **U5,** 57
nationality [næʃn'æləti] Staatsangehörigkeit, Nationalität **II**
nature ['neɪtʃə] Natur **U5,** 46
near [nɪə] nahe, in der Nähe von **I**
need [ni:d] brauchen **II**
nervous ['nɜːvəs] nervös, aufgeregt **II**
network ['netwɜːk] Netz, Netzwerk **U2,** 20
never ['nevə] nie, niemals **I**
new [njuː] neu **I**
newspaper ['njuːspeɪpə] Zeitung ⟨**U5,** 57⟩; **U8,** 77
next [nekst] nächster/nächste/nächstes **II**
next time ['nekst taɪm] nächstes Mal **U4,** 42
next to ['neks tʊ] neben **I**
nice [naɪs] nett, schön **I**
Nice to meet you. [naɪs tʊ 'mi:t ju:] Schön dich kennen zu lernen. **I**
night [naɪt] Nacht **II**
no [nəʊ] kein/keine **II**
no [nəʊ] nein **I**
nobody ['nəʊbədi] niemand, keiner **II**
noise [nɔɪz] Geräusch, Lärm **I**
north [nɔːθ] Norden **I**
Norwegian [nɔː'wiːdʒən] Norwegisch **II**
not [nɒt] nicht **I**
not … any ['nɒt 'eni] kein/keine **II**

not … anything ['nɒt 'eniθɪŋ] nichts II
not yet [nɒt 'jet] noch nicht U5, 48
notes [nəʊts] Notizen U1, 9
take notes [teɪk 'nəʊts] Notizen machen U1, 9
November [nəʊ'vembə] November I
now [naʊ] jetzt, nun I
number ['nʌmbə] Nummer I; Zahl II
nurse [nɜːs] Krankenpfleger/ Krankenschwester I

O

October [ɒk'təʊbə] Oktober I
of [ɒv] von I
of course [ɒv 'kɔːs] natürlich, selbstverständlich II
office ['ɒfɪs] Büro II
often ['ɒfn] oft I
oh [əʊ] null I
Oh. [əʊ] Oh. I
OK [əʊ'keɪ] OK, in Ordnung I
old [əʊld] alt I
How old are you? [haʊ 'əʊld ɑː juː] Wie alt bist du? I
on [ɒn] am, auf I
on Sunday [ɒn 'sʌndeɪ] am Sonntag; sonntags I
on the internet [ɒn ði 'ɪntənet] im Internet II
on the programme [ɒn ðə 'prəʊgræm] in der Sendung I
on the train [ɒn ðə 'treɪn] im Zug U1, 12
once [wʌns] einmal; einst U8, 78
once a week [wʌns ə 'wiːk] einmal pro Woche U8, 78
one [wʌn] eins I; ein/eine II
one hundred [wʌn'hʌndrəd] hundert II
one thousand [wʌn 'θaʊznd] tausend II
online [ɒn'laɪn] online II
only ['əʊnli] nur I
open ['əʊpn] öffnen I
open ['əʊpn] offen, geöffnet I
opposite ['ɒpəzɪt] gegenüber (von) I
or [ɔː] oder I
orange juice ['ɒrɪndʒ 'dʒuːs] Orangensaft I
orchestra ['ɔːkɪstrə] Orchester U6, 59
order ['ɔːdə] Reihenfolge U1, 13
order ['ɔːdə] bestellen U5, 48

organize ['ɔːgənaɪz] organisieren, koordinieren, veranstalten U4, 42
other ['ʌðə] anderer/andere/ anderes I
ought to ['ɔːt tʊ] sollte/sollten (besser) U1, 11
our ['aʊə] unser/unsere I
ourselves [aʊə'selvz] selbst, wir selbst, uns selbst U7, 70
out of ['aʊt əv] aus … heraus II
outside [aʊt'saɪd] außen, draußen, außerhalb I
over ['əʊvə] über I
own [əʊn] eigener/eigene/ eigenes I

P

pack [pæk] einpacken, packen II
page [peɪdʒ] Seite U2, 20
palace ['pælɪs] Palast U1, 8
⟨a sheet of paper⟩ [ə ʃiːt əv 'peɪpə] ein Stück Papier U3, 37
parents ['peərənts] Eltern I
park [pɑːk] Park I
part [pɑːt] Teil I
partner ['pɑːtnə] Partner/ Partnerin I
party ['pɑːti] Party I
have a party [hæv ə 'pɑːti] eine Party feiern, eine Party machen I
past [pɑːst] nach I
half past [hɑːf 'pɑːst] halb I
quarter past ['kwɔːtə pɑːst] viertel nach I
pasta ['pæstə] Teigwaren, Nudeln II
path [pɑːθ] Pfad, Weg I
pay, paid, paid [peɪ, peɪd, peɪd] zahlen, bezahlen U2, 20
PE [piː 'iː] Sportunterricht II
pea [piː] Erbse II
pen [pen] Füller I
pencil ['pentsl] Bleistift I
pencil case ['pentsl keɪs] Federmäppchen I
penny pl. pence ['peni, pi:] Pence (britische Währungseinheit) U2, 20
people ['piːpl] Leute, Menschen I
per [pɜː] pro U2, 20
percent [pə'sent] Prozent U8, 79
⟨period of time⟩ [pɪəriəd əv 'taɪm] Zeitraum U7, 75
person ['pɜːsn] Person U5, 47
pet [pet] Haustier I

phone [fəʊn] Telefon U1, 12
phone box ['fəʊn bɒks] Telefonzelle U2, 21
phone call ['fəʊn kɔːl] Telefongespräch, Anruf U2, 20
phone [fəʊn] anrufen I
photo ['fəʊtəʊ] Foto, Fotografie I
picture ['pɪktʃə] Bild I
take a picture [teɪk ə 'pɪktʃə] fotografieren, ein Foto machen II
pig [pɪg] Schwein I
⟨pillowcase⟩ ['pɪləʊkeɪs] Kissenbezug U5, 57
pilot ['paɪlət] Pilot/Pilotin U7, 67
pink [pɪŋk] pink, rosa I
pit [pɪt] Grube, Mine U3, 29
It's a pity. [ɪts ə 'pɪti] Es ist schade./Es ist bedauerlich. U7, 67
pizza ['piːtsə] Pizza II
place [pleɪs] Ort, Platz, Stelle II
plan [plæn] Plan I; Programm U2, 20
plan [plæn] planen U4, 42
plane [pleɪn] Flugzeug II
play [pleɪ] Spiel, Theaterstück I
play [pleɪ] spielen I
play a trick on somebody [pleɪ ə 'trɪk ɒn 'sʌmbədi] jemand einen Streich spielen II
player ['pleɪə] Spieler/Spielerin I
⟨pleasant⟩ ['pleznt] angenehm U7, 75
please [pliːz] bitte I
pocket ['pɒkɪt] Hosentasche, Jackentasche II
point [pɔɪnt] Punkt U3, 33
police pl. police [pə'liːs] Polizei I
police officer [pə'liːs 'ɒfɪsə] Polizist/Polizistin I
pond [pɒnd] Teich I
pony ['pəʊni] Pony I
pop concert ['pɒp kɒnsət] Popkonzert II
pop star ['pɒp stɑː] Popstar I
popular ['pɒpjələ] populär, beliebt U6, 60
position [pə'zɪʃn] Platz, Position U3, 33
post office ['pəʊst ɒfɪs] Postamt I
postcard ['pəʊstkɑːd] Postkarte, Ansichtskarte II
poster ['pəʊstə] Poster I
potato [pə'teɪtəʊ] Kartoffel II
pound [paʊnd] Pfund (britische Währungseinheit) I

practise ['præktɪs] üben **I**
prefer [prɪ'fɜ:] vorziehen, bevorzugen **U8**, 76
present ['preznt] Geschenk **I**
present [prɪ'zent] präsentieren, vorstellen **U4**, 42
presentation [preznteɪʃn] Präsentation **U2**, 24
pretty ['prɪti] hübsch **II**
princess [prɪn'ses] Prinzessin **II**
print out [prɪnt 'aʊt] ausdrucken **II**
⟨**prison**⟩ ['prɪzn] Gefängnis **U5**, 57
private ['praɪvɪt] privat **II**
prize [praɪz] Preis, Gewinn **I**
probably ['prɒbəbli] wahrscheinlich **II**
problem ['prɒbləm] Problem **I**
procession [prə'seʃn] Umzug, Festzug **I**
profile ['prəʊfaɪl] (Zeugnis mit Selbstbeurteilung) **U4**, 39; Porträt, Profil **U6**, 62
programme ['prəʊɡræm] Sendung **I**
on the programme [ɒn ðə 'prəʊɡræm] in der Sendung **I**
project ['prɒdʒekt] Projekt **I**
project day ['prɒdʒekt deɪ] Projekttag **I**
⟨**protect**⟩ [prə'tekt] schützen **U1**, 19; **U7**, 75
pull [pʊl] ziehen **U7**, 67
⟨**pull apart**⟩ [pʊl ə'pɑːt] auseinander ziehen **U3**, 37
pupil ['pjuːpl] Schüler/Schülerin **I**
push [pʊʃ] stoßen, schieben **II**
put, put, put [pʊt, pʊt, pʊt] setzen, stellen, legen **I**; hineintun, stecken **II**; laden **II**
puzzle ['pʌzl] Rätsel **U1**, 17

Q

quarter past ['kwɔːtə pɑːst] viertel nach **I**
queen [kwiːn] Königin **U1**, 8
question ['kwestʃən] Frage **I**
questionnaire [kwestʃə'neə] Fragebogen **U6**, 59
quick [kwɪk] schnell **I**
quiet ['kwaɪət] leise **I**
Be quiet. [bi: 'kwaɪət] Sei/Seid leise. **I**
quite [kwaɪt] ziemlich, ganz **U4**, 39
quiz [kwɪz] Quiz **I**

R

rabbit ['ræbɪt] Kaninchen **I**
race [reɪs] Rennen **I**
radio ['reɪdiəʊ] Radio **I**
rain [reɪn] Regen **U7**, 65
rain [reɪn] regnen **U5**, 46
rainy ['reɪni] regnerisch, verregnet **I**
⟨**raise**⟩ [reɪz] anheben **U5**, 57
read, read, read [riːd, red, red] lesen **I**
read music [riːd 'mjuːzɪk] Noten lesen **U6**, 59
ready ['redi] fertig **I**
⟨**realize**⟩ ['rɪəlaɪz] bemerken **U5**, 57
really ['rɪəli] wirklich **I**
⟨**reception**⟩ [rɪ'sepʃn] Empfang, Rezeption **U2**, 25
⟨**recognize**⟩ ['rekəgnaɪz] erkennen **U5**, 57
recorder [rɪ'kɔːdə] Blockflöte **U6**, 59
red [red] rot **I**
registration [redʒɪ'streɪʃn] Anwesenheitskontrolle **II**
relax [rɪ'læks] entspannen, sich beruhigen **II**
remember [rɪ'membə] denken an, sich erinnern **II**
remind somebody [rɪ'maɪnd sʌmbədi] jemanden erinnern **U6**, 59
remote control [rɪməʊt kən'trəʊl] Fernsteuerung, Fernbedienung **U5**, 51
repair [rɪ'peə] reparieren **I**
report [rɪ'pɔːt] Zeugnis, Bericht **U4**, 39
reporter [rɪ'pɔːtə] Reporter/Reporterin **I**
restaurant ['restrɑːŋ] Restaurant, Gaststätte **I**
result [rɪ'zʌlt] Ergebnis, Resultat **I**
rice [raɪs] Reis **II**
ride, rode, ridden [raɪd, rəʊd, 'rɪdn] fahren, reiten **U5**, 46
right [raɪt] richtig **I**; rechts **I**
be right [bi: 'raɪt] Recht haben **II**
on the right [ɒn ðə 'raɪt] rechts **I**
ring, rang, rung [rɪŋ, ræŋ, rʌŋ] klingeln, läuten **II**
ring tone ['rɪŋ təʊn] Klingelton **U2**, 20
river ['rɪvə] Fluss **I**
road [rəʊd] Straße **I**
robot ['rəʊbɒt] Roboter **I**
⟨**roll up**⟩ [rəʊl 'ʌp] aufrollen **U3**, 37

room [ruːm] Zimmer, Raum **I**
route [ruːt] Strecke, Route **U5**, 46
go **rowing** [ɡəʊ 'rəʊɪŋ] rudern gehen **II**
rowing club ['rəʊɪŋ klʌb] Ruderclub **II**
rubber ['rʌbə] Radiergummi **I**
rucksack ['rʌksæk] Rucksack **I**
rule [ruːl] Regel **I**
ruler ['ruːlə] Lineal **I**
run, ran, run [rʌn, ræn, rʌn] laufen, rennen **I**
ran away: I ran away [ræn ə'weɪ] ich lief weg/ich bin weggelaufen **II**
ran into: I ran into [ræn 'ɪntə] ich lief in …hinein/ich bin in … hineingelaufen **II**
run from ['rʌn frɒm] weglaufen vor **I**

S

sad [sæd] traurig, schmerzlich **I**
salad ['sæləd] Salat **II**
the **same** [seɪm] derselbe/dieselbe/dasselbe **I**
sanction ['sæŋkʃn] Sanktion, Strafe **U4**, 40
⟨**sand**⟩ [sænd] Sand **U1**, 19
⟨**sandstorm**⟩ ['sændstɔːm] Sandsturm **U1**, 19
sandwich ['sænwɪdʒ] Sandwich, belegtes Brot **I**
Saturday ['sætədeɪ] Samstag **I**
save [seɪv] retten **U7**, 67
say, said, said [seɪ, sed, sed] sagen **I**
say hello [seɪ he'ləʊ] Grüße ausrichten **II**
be **scared** [bi: 'skeəd] Angst haben, verängstigt sein **II**
school [skuːl] Schule **I**
school team [skuːl 'tiːm] Schulmannschaft **I**
Science ['saɪəns] Naturwissenschaft, Wissenschaft **II**
Scottish ['skɒtɪʃ] schottisch **U5**, 46
scream [skriːm] schreien **II**
sea [siː] Meer **II**
secret ['siːkrət] Geheimnis **II**
security guard [se'kjʊərəti ɡɑːd] Wachmann/Wachfrau **II**
see, saw, seen [siː, sɔː, siːn] sehen **I**
See you there. [siː jə 'ðeə] Wir sehen uns dort. **I**

sell, sold, sold [sel, səʊld, səʊld] verkaufen **I**
send, sent, sent [send, sent, sent] schicken, senden **I**
sentence ['sentəns] Satz **U1**, 11
September [sep'tembə] September **I**
she [ʃiː] sie **I**
shed [ʃed] Schuppen **I**
sheep pl. **sheep** [ʃiːp] Schaf **I**
⟨a sheet of paper⟩ [ə ʃiːt əv 'peɪpə] ein Stück Papier **U3**, 37
ship [ʃɪp] Schiff **II**
shirt [ʃɜːt] Hemd **II**
shocked [ʃɒkt] schockiert, erschüttert **U6**, 60
shoe [ʃuː] Schuh **I**
shop [ʃɒp] Laden, Geschäft **I**
go **shopping** [gəʊ 'ʃɒpɪŋ] einkaufen gehen **II**
short [ʃɔːt] kurz **II**
should [ʃʊd] sollte/sollten **II**
you should [ju ʃʊd] du solltest **II**
shout [ʃaʊt] schreien, rufen **II**
shout at [ʃaʊt 'æt] anschreien **II**
show [ʃəʊ] zeigen **I**
sight [saɪt] Sehenswürdigkeit **U1**, 8
sign [saɪn] Schild, Zeichen **U7**, 71
simulator ['sɪmjəleɪtə] Simulator **II**
sing, sang, sung [sɪŋ, sæŋ, sʌŋ] singen **I**
singer ['sɪŋə] Sänger/Sängerin **II**
⟨sink into⟩ [sɪŋk 'ɪntə] einsinken **U1**, 19
sister ['sɪstə] Schwester **I**
sit, sat, sat [sɪt, sæt, sæt] sitzen **I**
sat down: I sat down [sæt 'daʊn] ich setzte mich hin/ich habe mich hingesetzt **II**
situation [sɪtjuˈeɪʃn] Situation, Lage **U4**, 41
skateboard ['skeɪtbɔːd] Skateboard **I**
ski [skiː] Ski **II**
ski jump ['skiː dʒʌmp] Sprungschanze **II**
skirt [skɜːt] Rock **I**
sleep, slept, slept [sliːp, slept, slept] schlafen **I**
sleeping bag ['sliːpɪŋ bæg] Schlafsack **I**
slow [sləʊ] langsam **II**
slowly ['sləʊli] langsam **II**
small [smɔːl] klein **I**

smelly ['smeli] stinkend **II**
snack [snæk] Imbiss, Snack **I**
snow [snəʊ] Schnee **U7**, 64
so [səʊ] so **I**
so [səʊ] also, folglich **I**; deshalb, daher **II**
sofa ['səʊfə] Sofa **I**
⟨soft⟩ [sɒft] weich **U1**, 19
some [sʌm] einige, etwas **I**; ein paar **II**
somebody ['sʌmbədi] jemand **II**
something ['sʌmθɪŋ] etwas **II**
sometimes ['sʌmtaɪmz] manchmal **I**
son [sʌn] Sohn **II**
song [sɒŋ] Lied **I**
soon [suːn] bald **I**
I'm **sorry.** [aɪm 'sɒri] Tut mir Leid. **I**
sound [saʊnd] Laut, Ton **U5**, 55
south [saʊθ] Süden **I**
southwest [saʊθ'west] südwestlich, Südwest- **I**
speak, spoke, spoken [spiːk, spəʊk, 'spəʊkn] sprechen **I**
Speak to you later. [spiːk tə jə 'leɪtə] Bis dann. **U2**, 21
This is ... speaking. ['ðɪs ɪz ... 'spiːkɪŋ] Hier spricht ..., Hier ist ... . **II**
speaker ['spiːkə] Sprecher **U7**, 70
special ['speʃl] besonderer/besondere/besonderes **I**
spectator [spek'teɪtə] Zuschauer/Zuschauerin **U8**, 76
spectator sport [spek'teɪtə spɔːt] Publikumssport **U8**, 76
spelling ['spelɪŋ] Rechtschreibung **U5**, 55
spicy ['spaɪsi] scharf, stark gewürzt **II**
spider ['spaɪdə] Spinne **I**
split, split, split [splɪt, splɪt, splɪt] sich trennen **U6**, 60
sponge [spʌndʒ] Schwamm **I**
spoon [spuːn] Löffel **II**
sports [spɔːts] Sport **I**
do sports [du: 'spɔːts] Sport(-arten) treiben **I**
sports field ['spɔːts fiːld] Sportplatz **I**
sports hall ['spɔːts hɔːl] Turnhalle **I**
spring [sprɪŋ] Frühling **I**
stairs [steəz] Treppe **II**
stall [stɔːl] Bude, Stand **I**
stand, stood, stood [stænd, stʊd, stʊd] stehen **I**
star [stɑː] Star, Stern **I**

start [stɑːt] anfangen **I**
station ['steɪʃn] Haltestelle, Bahnhof **U1**, 12
⟨stay⟩ [steɪ] Aufenthalt **U7**, 75
stay [steɪ] wohnen, übernachten **I**; bleiben **II**
steal, stole, stolen [stiːl, stəʊl, 'stəʊlən] stehlen **U2**, 22
step [step] Schritt **U8**, 80
still [stɪl] noch **I**
stop [stɒp] aufhören **II**
storm [stɔːm] Sturm **U7**, 65
story ['stɔːri] Geschichte **II**
straight on [streɪt 'ɒn] geradeaus **I**
strange [streɪndʒ] seltsam, sonderbar, merkwürdig **II**
strategy ['strætədʒi] Strategie, Lerntechnik **U2**, 25
street [striːt] Straße **I**
stress [stres] Stress, Belastung **I**
stressed [strest] gestresst, belastet **I**
strict [strɪkt] streng **II**
style [staɪl] Stil, Art **II**
subject ['sʌbdʒɪkt] Schulfach **II**
⟨such⟩ [sʌtʃ] so **U1**, 19
suddenly ['sʌdnli] plötzlich **II**
sugar ['ʃʊgə] Zucker **II**
summer ['sʌmə] Sommer **I**
Sunday ['sʌndeɪ] Sonntag **I**
on Sunday [ɒn 'sʌndeɪ] am Sonntag; sonntags **I**
sunny ['sʌni] sonnig, heiter **I**
sure [ʃɔː] sicher **I**
surf [sɜːf] surfen **II**
surfing ['sɜːfɪŋ] Surfen **II**
go surfing [gəʊ 'sɜːfɪŋ] surfen gehen **II**
survey ['sɜːveɪ] Umfrage **I**
sweatshirt ['swetʃɜːt] Sweatshirt **I**
swim, swam, swum [swɪm, swæm, swʌm] schwimmen **U2**, 23
swimmer ['swɪmə] Schwimmer/Schwimmerin **II**
go **swimming** [gəʊ 'swɪmɪŋ] schwimmen gehen **I**
swimming pool ['swɪmɪŋ puːl] Schwimmbad **I**
switch off [swɪtʃ 'ɒf] ausschalten **U2**, 22

T

table ['teɪbl] Tisch **I**
take, took, taken [teɪk, tʊk, 'teɪkn] nehmen, mitnehmen **I**; nehmen, mit ... fahren **I**; abholen **II**; bringen **II**

take a picture [teɪk ə 'pɪktʃə] fotografieren, ein Foto machen **II**

take notes [teɪk 'nəʊts] Notizen machen **U1,** 9

take part in [teɪk 'pɑːt ɪn] teilnehmen an **I**

take the times [teɪk ðə 'taɪmz] die Zeiten messen **I**

takeaway ['teɪkəweɪ] Mitnahmerestaurant, Essen zum Mitnehmen **II**

talk [tɔːk] sprechen, reden **II**

talk about [tɔːk ə'baʊt] sprechen über, reden über **I**

talk to ['tɔːk tʊ] sprechen mit, reden mit **I**

tall [tɔːl] groß, hoch **II**

taxi ['tæksi] Taxi **I**

tea [tiː] Tee **I**

teach, taught, taught [tiːtʃ, tɔːt, tɔːt] unterrichten **I**

teacher ['tiːtʃə] Lehrer/Lehrerin **I**

team [tiːm] Mannschaft, Team **I**

⟨**teenager**⟩ ['tiːneɪdʒə] Teenager **U2,** 25

telephone ['telɪfəʊn] Telefon **I**

television ['telɪvɪʒn] Fernseher **I**

tell, told, told [tel, təʊld, təʊld] sagen, erzählen **I**

tell about [tel ə'baʊt] erzählen von **II**

temperature ['temprətʃə] Temperatur **U7,** 64

temple ['templ] Tempel **U1,** 9

tennis ['tenɪs] Tennis **I**

tent [tent] Zelt **I**

term [tɜːm] Trimester, Semester **I**

test [test] Test, Klassenarbeit **II**

text [tekst] Text **I**

text message ['tekst 'mesɪdʒ] SMS **II**

text [tekst] eine SMS schreiben **U2,** 20

Text me back. [tekst mi: 'bæk] Schreib zurück (SZ). **II**

than [ðæn] als **II**

thank you ['θæŋkjuː] danke (schön) **I**

Fine, thanks. ['faɪn θæŋks] Danke, gut. **I**

that [ðæt] dass **II**

that [ðæt] das; jener/jene/jenes **I**

That's that! [ðæts 'ðæt] Damit basta! **I**

that [ðæt] der/die/das; dem/

den *(Relativpronomen)* **U6,** 58

the [ðə, ðiː] der/die/das **I**

the most embarrassing [ðə məʊst ɪm'bærəsɪŋ] der/die/das peinlichste, der/die/das unangenehmste **II**

the next morning [ðə nekst 'mɔːnɪŋ] am nächsten Morgen **U3,** 31

the same [seɪm] derselbe/dieselbe/dasselbe **I**

their [ðeə] ihr/ihre **I**

them [ðem] sie; ihnen **I**

themselves [ðem'selvz] selbst, sie selbst, sich selbst **U7,** 67

then [ðen] dann **I**

there [ðeə] da, dort **I**; da hin, dort hin **II**

in there [ɪn 'ðeə] da drin, dort drin **I**

See you there. [siː jə 'ðeə] Wir sehen uns dort. **I**

there are [ðeə 'ɑː] da sind **I**

there is [ðeə 'ɪz] da ist, es gibt, es ist **I**

these [ðiːz] diese **I**

they [ðeɪ] *(pl.)* sie **I**

They're ... . [ðeə] Sie kosten ... . **I**

thing [θɪŋ] Ding, Sache **I**

think, thought, thought [θɪŋk, θɔːt, θɔːt] finden, meinen, denken **I**

thirsty ['θɜːsti] durstig **I**

this [ðɪs] dieser/diese/dieses **I**

this is ['ðɪs ɪz] dies ist, das ist **I**

This is ... speaking. ['ðɪs ɪz ... 'spiːkɪŋ] Hier spricht ... ., Hier ist ... . **II**

this is why [ðɪs ɪz 'waɪ] deshalb **I**

this afternoon [ðɪs ɑːftə'nuːn] heute Nachmittag **U3,** 28

those [ðəʊz] jene **I**

thousands ['θaʊzəndz] tausende, viele tausend **U7,** 64

through [θruː] durch **U5,** 51

throw, threw, thrown [θrəʊ, θruː, θrəʊn] werfen **I**

Thursday ['θɜːzdeɪ] Donnerstag **I**

ticket ['tɪkɪt] Eintrittskarte, Ticket **I**

tidy up [taɪdi 'ʌp] aufräumen **II**

tidy ['taɪdi] ordentlich **I**

time [taɪm] Zeit **I**

next time ['nekst taɪm] nächstes Mal **U4,** 42

take the times [teɪk ðə 'taɪmz] die Zeiten messen **I**

What time ist it? [wɒt 'taɪm ɪz ɪt] Wie viel Uhr ist es? **I**

timetable ['taɪmteɪbl] Stundenplan **II**

tip [tɪp] Ratschlag, Tipp **U1,** 15; Spitze ⟨**U3,** 37⟩

tired ['taɪəd] müde **I**

title ['taɪtl] Titel, Überschrift **U6,** 60

to [tʊ] vor **I**; an, nach, zu **I**

to [tʊ] um zu **I**

toast [təʊst] Toast(brot) **I**

today [tə'deɪ] heute **I**

together [tə'geðə] zusammen **II**

toilet ['tɔɪlət] Toilette **I**

tomorrow [tə'mɒrəʊ] morgen **I**

⟨**ton**⟩ [tʌn] Tonne **U7,** 75

tonight [tə'naɪt] heute Abend, heute Nacht **U3,** 29

too [tuː] auch **I**; zu **I**

top [tɒp] oberer Teil, Spitze **II**

topic ['tɒpɪk] Thema **U2,** 20

torch [tɔːtʃ] Taschenlampe **I**

tornado [tɔː'neɪdəʊ] Tornado **U7,** 65

totally ['təʊtəli] total, völlig **U6,** 58

tour [tʊə] Führung, Tour **U3,** 32

tourist ['tʊərɪst] Tourist/Touristin **I**

⟨**towel**⟩ [taʊəl] Handtuch **U7,** 75

⟨**towel rack**⟩ [taʊəl 'ræk] Handtuchhalter **U7,** 75

tower ['taʊə] Turm **II**

town [taʊn] Stadt **I**

in town [ɪn 'taʊn] in der Stadt **I**

town centre [taʊn 'sentə] Stadtzentrum **U7,** 65

tractor ['træktə] Traktor **I**

train [treɪn] Zug **I**

on the train [ɒn ðə 'treɪn] im Zug **U1,** 12

train [treɪn] trainieren **I**

trainer ['treɪnə] Turnschuh **II**

training ['treɪnɪŋ] Training **U3,** 28

tree [triː] Baum **I**

trick [trɪk] Trick **I**

play a trick on somebody [pleɪ ə 'trɪk ɒn 'sʌmbədi] jemand einen Streich spielen **II**

trip [trɪp] Fahrt, Reise **U1,** 14

camping trip ['kæmpɪŋ trɪp] Campingausflug, Campingtrip **II** go on a trip [gəʊ ɒn ə 'trɪp] einen Ausflug machen, eine Reise machen **II**

trombone [trɒm'bəʊn] Posaune **U3**, 26

trouble ['trʌbl] Schwierigkeiten, Ärger **I**

trousers ['traʊzez] Hose **I**

true [truː] wahr **II**

trumpet ['trʌmpɪt] Trompete **U6**, 59

try [traɪ] versuchen, ausprobieren **I**

T-shirt ['tiːʃɜːt] T-Shirt **I**

Tuesday ['tjuːzdeɪ] Dienstag **I**

tunnel ['tʌnl] Tunnel, Unterführung **I**

turn [tɜːn] abbiegen **I**

tutor group ['tjuːtə gruːp] Klasse *(in einer englischen Schule)* **I**

TV [tiː'viː] Fernseher **I**

twenty-six [twenti 'sɪks] sechsundzwanzig **I**

⟨**twice**⟩ [twaɪs] zweimal **U7**, 75

twinned [twɪnd] verschwistert **U3**, 26

type [taɪp] Typ **U8**, 78

type in [taɪp 'ɪn] eingeben **II**

U

uncle ['ʌŋkl] Onkel **U1**, 8

under ['ʌndə] unter **I**

Underground ['ʌndəgraʊnd] U-Bahn **I**

understand, understood, understood [ʌndə'stænd, ʌndə'stʊd, ʌndə'stʊd] verstehen **II**

unhappy [ʌn'hæpi] unglücklich **U6**, 60

uniform ['juːnɪfɔːm] Uniform **I**

unit ['juːnɪt] Kapitel **U1**, 15

until [ʌn'tɪl] bis **II**

up [ʌp] hoch, hinauf **II**

upset [ʌp'set] bestürzt, aufgeregt **II**

us [ʌs] uns; wir **I**

use [juːz] benutzen, verwenden **II**

⟨**by using ...**⟩ [baɪ 'juːzɪŋ] indem Sie ... benutzen **U7**, 75

usually ['juːʒli] normalerweise, gewöhnlich **I**

V

valley ['væli] Tal **U7**, 66

van [væn] Lieferwagen, Kleintransporter **I**

vegetable ['vedʒtəbl] Gemüse **I**

vegetarian [vedʒɪ'teəriən] Vegetarier/Vegetarierin **II**

vegetarian [vedʒɪ'teəriən] vegetarisch **II**

very ['veri] sehr **I**

video camera ['vɪdiəʊ kæmrə] Videokamera, Camcorder **I**

Viking ['vaɪkɪŋ] Wikinger **II**

village ['vɪlɪdʒ] Dorf **II**

visit ['vɪzɪt] Besuch **I**

visit ['vɪzɪt] besuchen **I**; besichtigen **II**

voice [vɔɪs] Stimme **II**

volleyball ['vɒlibɔːl] Volleyball **I**

W

wait [weɪt] warten **I**

wait for [weɪt 'fɔː] warten auf **II**

walk [wɔːk] gehen, laufen **I**

wall [wɔːl] Wand ⟨**U3**, 37⟩; **U4**, 41

wallet ['wɒlɪt] Brieftasche **II**

want (to) ['wɒnt tʊ] wollen, mögen **I**

warm [wɔːm] warm **U7**, 64

wash [wɒʃ] waschen **I**

wash up [wɒʃ 'ʌp] abwaschen, abspülen **II**

⟨**waste**⟩ [weɪst] verschwenden **U7**, 75

watch [wɒtʃ] Armbanduhr **U3**, 30

watch [wɒtʃ] anschauen, zusehen **I**; beobachten **I**

water ['wɔːtə] Wasser **I**

way [weɪ] Art, Weg, Methode **U2**, 24

we [wiː] wir **I**

wear, wore, worn *(Kleidung)* [weə, wɔː, wɔːn] anhaben, tragen **I**

weather ['weðə] Wetter **I**

web [web] Netz, Netzwerk **U1**, 16

website ['websaɪt] Website **II**

wedding ['wedɪŋ] Hochzeit **U1**, 9

Wednesday ['wenzdeɪ] Mittwoch **I**

week [wiːk] Woche **I**

weekend [wiːk'end] Wochenende **I**

at the weekend [æt ðe wiːk'end] am Wochenende **I**

welcome ['welkʌm] willkommen **U3**, 26

You're welcome. [jɔː 'welkəm] Bitte./Gern geschehen. **I**

well [wel] gut **U3**, 30

well [wel] nun (ja) **II**

Welsh [welʃ] walisisch; Waliser/Waliserin **U3**, 26

west [west] Westen **I**

West Indian [west 'ɪndiən] westindisch; Westinder/Westinderin **U1**, 12

wet [wet] nass **II**

what [wɒt] was **I**; welcher/welche/welches **I**

What colour is ... ? [wɒt 'kʌlər ɪz] Welche Farbe hat ... ? **I**

What's happening? [wɒts 'hæpenɪŋ] Was geht hier vor? **I**

What's ... like? ['wɒts 'laɪk] Wie ist ...? **II**

What's missing? [wɒts 'mɪsɪŋ] Was fehlt? **U1**, 10

What's the matter? [wɒts ðe 'mætə] Was ist los? **II**

What's wrong? [wɒts 'rɒŋ] Was ist los? **I**

What's your name? [wɒts jɔː 'neɪm] Wie heißt du? **I**

⟨What the heck ...?⟩ [wɒt ðə 'hek] Was, zum Teufel ...? **U1**, 19

What time is it? [wɒt 'taɪm ɪz ɪt] Wie viel Uhr ist es? **I**

when [wen] wenn **II**; als **II**

when [wen] wann **I**

where [weə] wo **I**; wohin **I**

Where are you from? [weər ɑː jə 'frɒm] Woher kommst du? **I**

which [wɪtʃ] welcher/welche/welches **I**

white [waɪt] weiß **II**

who [huː] wer **I**

⟨**whole**⟩ [həʊl] ganz **U5**, 57

why [waɪ] warum **I**

this is why [ðɪs ɪz 'waɪ] deshalb **I**

wide [waɪd] breit **II**

wild [waɪld] wild **I**

will [wɪl] werden **II**

won't [wəʊnt] nicht werden **II**

win, won, won [wɪn, wʌn, wʌn] gewinnen **I**

wind [wɪnd] Wind **U7**, 65

window ['wɪndəʊ] Fenster **I**

winter ['wɪntə] Winter **I**

witch [wɪtʃ] Hexe **U7**, 68

witchcraft ['wɪtʃkrɑːft] Hexerei **U7**, 66

with [wɪð] mit, mit ... zusammen, bei **I**

without [wɪ'ðaʊt] ohne **II**
woman pl. **women** ['wʊmən; 'wɪmɪn] Frau **II**
word [wɜːd] Wort **I**
work [wɜːk] Arbeit **I**
work [wɜːk] arbeiten **I**; funktionieren **I**
worksheet ['wɜːkʃiːt] Arbeitsblatt **I**
worried ['wʌrid] beunruhigt, besorgt **I**
worse [wɜːs] schlechter, schlimmer **II**
the **worst** [wɜːst] der/die/das schlechteste, der/die/das schlimmste **II**
I'd like to .... [aɪd 'laɪk tʊ] Ich würde gerne ...., Ich möchte .... **I**
Would you like ... ? [wʊd jə 'laɪk] Möchtest du ... ?/ Möchten Sie ... ? **I**
write, wrote, written [raɪt, rəʊt, 'rɪtn] schreiben **I**
wrong [rɒŋ] falsch **I**
be wrong [bi: 'rɒŋ] Unrecht haben **U2**, 23
What's wrong? [wɒts 'rɒŋ] Was ist los? **I**

Y

yeah [jeə] ja **II**
year [jɪə] Jahr **I**
Year 7 [jɪə 'sevn] Klasse sieben **I**
yellow ['jeləʊ] gelb **I**
yes [jes] ja **I**
yesterday ['jestədeɪ] gestern **II**
yet [jet] schon, noch **II**
not yet [nɒt 'jet] noch nicht **U5**, 48
yoga ['jəʊgə] Yoga **II**
yoghurt ['jɒgət] Joghurt **II**
you [juː] du **I**; ihr **I**; dir; dich **I**; euch **I**; man **II**
you should [ju 'ʃʊd] du solltest **II**
You're welcome. [jɔː 'welkəm] Bitte./Gern geschehen. **I**
young [jʌŋ] jung **I**
⟨youngster⟩ ['jʌŋstə] Jugendliche/Jugendlicher **U1**, 19
your [jɔː] dein/deine **I**; euer/eure, Ihr/Ihre **I**
yourself [jɔː'self] selbst, du selbst, dich selbst **U7**, 67
youth hostel ['juːθ hɒstl] Jugendherberge **U5**, 47

Z

zoo [zuː] Zoo **II**

Boys' names

Alex ['ælɪks] **U6**, 58
Andrew ['ændruː] **U5**, 48
Andy ['ændi] **I**
Ashraf ['æʃrəv] **U8**, 76
Ben [ben] **I**
Brad [bræd] **II**
Charles [tʃɑːlz] **II**
Dan [dæn] **I**
Fred [fred] **U1**, 10
Jake [dʒeɪk] **II**
Lars [lɑːz] **II**
Leroy ['liːrɔɪ] **II**
Luke [luːk] **I**
Mark [mɑːk] **I**
Matt [mæt] **I**
Max [mæks] ⟨**U4**, 43⟩; **U7**, 71
Peter ['piːtə] **I**
Rhodri ['rɒdri] **U3**, 27
Richard ['rɪtʃəd] **I**
Sam [sæm] **I**
Scott [skɒt] **I**
Simon ['saɪmən] **I**
Sridhar ['srɪdhɑː] **II**
Steven ['stiːvn] **I**
Sven [sven] **II**
Terry ['teri] **I**
Tim [tɪm] **I**
Tom [tɒm] **I**
Tommy ['tɒmi] **U6**, 62

Girls' names

Alexandra [ælɪg'zɑːndrə] **U4**, 38
Anna ['ænə] **I**
Barbara ['bɑːbrə] **II**
Claire [kleə] **U6**, 58
Eleanor ['elɪnə] **II**
Emma ['emə] **I**
Eva ['iːvə] **I**
Farah ['fɑːrə] **I**
Francesca [fræn'tʃeskə] **U2**, 23
Gemma ['dʒemə] **II**
Helen ['helən] **I**
Jade [dʒeɪd] **I**
Jenny ['dʒeni] **I**
Karita [kʌ'riːtʌ] **II**
Kate [keɪt] **U7**, 67
Katie ['keɪti] **I**
Kelly ['keli] **U6**, 60
Kerry ['keri] **U3**, 26
Linda ['lɪndə] **I**
Lisa ['liːsə] **I**
Louise [luː'iːz] **U1**, 14

Lucy ['luːsi] **U5**, 53
Margaret ['mɑːgrət] **II**
Meg [meg] **I**
Naomi ['neɪəmi] **U4**, 42
Nasreen [nʌs'riːn] **I**
Nicky ['nɪki] **U8**, 78
Nina ['niːnə] **I**
Sarah ['seərə] **II**
Sonja ['sɒnjə] **II**
Sue [suː] **U7**, 71
Susan ['suːzn] **I**
Susie ['suːzi] **I**
Tammy ['tæmi] **U5**, 52
Tara ['tɑːrə] **I**
Ulrika [ʊl'riːkʌ] **II**

Surnames

Baker ['beɪkə] **II**
Barnes [bɑːnz] **U4**, 39
Beckham ['bekəm] **II**
Benson ['bensn] **U7**, 68
Bray [breɪ] **I**
Brook [brʊk] **I**
Brown [braʊn] **I**
Burns [bɜːnz] **U5**, 45
Carter ['kɑːtə] **I**
Clark [klɑːk] **I**
Cook [kʊk] **II**
Harvey ['hɑːvi] **I**
Hu [huː] **I**
Jackson ['dʒæksən] **I**
Jones [dʒəʊnz] **U3**, 27
McWilliams [mək'wɪljəmz] **U5**, 48
Newman ['njuːmən] **I**
Olsen ['əʊlsən] **II**
Penford ['penfɔːd] **I**
Richards ['rɪtʃədz] **I**
Rose [rəʊz] **I**
Spencer ['spentsə] **I**
Stone [stəʊn] **II**
Taylor ['teɪlə] **I**
Uddin ['ʌdɪn] **II**
Webb [web] **I**
⟨**Wilder**⟩ ['waɪldə] **U5**, 57
Williams ['wɪljəmz] **I**

Place names

Abergavenny [æbəgə'veni] **U3**, 26
America [ə'merɪkə] **U1**, 8
⟨**Arkansas**⟩ ['ɑːkənsɔː] **U5**, 57
Australia [ɒs'treɪlɪə] **II**
Baker Street ['beɪkə striːt] **U1**, 15
Ben Nevis [ben 'nevɪs] **U5**, 46
Berlin [bɜː'lɪn] **I**
Birmingham ['bɜːmɪŋəm] **U6**, 60

Boscastle ['bɒskɑːsl] **U7**, 66
Bristol ['brɪstl] **U6**, 60
Cardiff ['kɑːdɪf] **U6**, 60
Carmarthen [kəˈmɑːðən]
U3, 30
Cornwall ['kɔːnwɔːl] **U7**, 66
Crane Street ['kreɪn striːt] **I**
Dartmoor ['dɑːtmɔː] **I**
Devon ['devn] **I**
Dorset ['dɔːsɪt] **II**
Edinburgh ['edɪnbrə] **U5**, 46
England ['ɪŋglənd] **I**
Europe ['jʊərəp] **U1**, 9
Germany ['dʒɜːməni] **I**
Greenwich ['grenɪdʒ] **I**
Greenwich Market [grenɪdʒ
'mɑːkɪt] **I**
Greenwich Road [grenɪdʒ
'rəʊd] **I**
Hither Farm Road [hɪðə fɑːm
'rəʊd] **I**
Holburn Road [hɒlbɜːn 'rəʊd] **I**
India ['ɪndɪə] **I**
Italy ['ɪtli] **II**
King William Walk [kɪŋ wɪljəm
'wɔːk] **I**
Loch Ness [lɒk 'nes] **U5**, 46
London ['lʌndən] **I**
London Road [lʌndən 'rəʊd] **I**
Manchester ['mæntʃɪstə]
U8, 76
Mars [mɑːz] **II**
Monmouth Town [mɒnməθ
'taʊn] **U3**, 32
Nelson Road [nelsn 'rəʊd] **I**
Newtown ['njuːtaʊn] **U3**, 32
New York [njuːˈjɔːk] **I**
Norway ['nɔːweɪ] **II**
Oslo ['ɒzləʊ] **II**
Oxford Street ['ɒksfəd striːt] **II**
Park Row [pɑːk 'rəʊ] **I**
Piccadilly Circus [pɪkədɪli
'sɜːkəs] **U1**, 13
River Thames [rɪvə 'temz] **I**
Rogestone ['rɒdʒəstən] **U3**, 32
Romney Road [rɒmni 'rəʊd] **I**
Scotland ['skɒtlənd] **U5**, 46
Stonehenge [stəʊn'hendʒ] **II**
Trafalgar Square [trəfælgə
'skweə] **U1**, 13
Turkey ['tɜːki] **II**
UK (United Kingdom) [juːˈkeɪ,
juːnaɪtɪd 'kɪŋdəm] **U2**, 20
Wales [weɪlz] **U3**, 26

Wendover Road [wendəʊvə
'rəʊd] **I**
West End [west 'end] **U1**, 9

Other names

A. C. Pontymiste [eɪsi:
pɒntɪ'mɪst] **U3**, 32
Bakerloo Line ['beɪkəluː laɪn]
U1, 15
Barker ['bɑːkə] **I**
Beatles ['biːtlz] **I**
Big Ben [bɪg 'ben] **U1**, 15
Big Pit [bɪg 'pɪt] **U3**, 29
Blue Note Café [bluː nəʊt
'kæfeɪ] **I**
Brad Pitt [bræd 'pɪt] **I**
Britney Spears [brɪtni 'spɪəz] **II**
Buckingham Palace [bʌkɪŋəm
'pælɪs] **U1**, 8
Bugsy Malone [bʌgzi
mə'ləʊn] **I**
Burger Bar ['bɜːgə bɑː] **I**
Café Mambo [kæfeɪ
'mæmbəʊ] **U1**, 13
Canary Wharf tower [kəneəri
wɔːf 'taʊə] **II**
Carmarthen Castle [kəmɑːθən
'kɑːsl] **U3**, 30
Central Line ['sentrl laɪn]
U1, 12
Charing Cross [tʃærɪŋ 'krɒs]
U1, 15
Chicago Bulls [ʃɪkɑːgəʊ 'bʊlz] **II**
Childline ['tʃaɪldlaɪn] **U4**, 42
Circle Line ['sɜːkl laɪn] **U1**, 15
Cutty Sark [kʌti 'sɑːk] **I**
Dartmoor Safaris [dɑːtmɔː
sə'fɑːriz] **I**
David Bowie [deɪvɪd 'baʊi] **I**
Eastlife ['iːstlaɪf] **II**
Formula One [fɔːmjələ 'wʌn] **I**
Galaxy Radio [gæləksi 'reɪ-
diəʊ] **I**
Garden Restaurant [gɑːdn
'restrɑːŋ] **I**
Greendale Farm [griːndeɪl
'fɑːm] **I**
Greenwich Mean Time
[grenɪdʒ 'miːn taɪm] **I**
Javine [dʒə'viːn] **U6**, 58
Kensington ['kenzɪŋtən]
U1, 15

London Eye [lʌndən 'aɪ] **U1**, 10
London Marathon [lʌndən
'mærəθn] **II**
Manchester United [mæntʃɪstə
juːˈnaɪtɪd] **U3**, 27
Matrix ['meɪtrɪks] **U6**, 60
McFly [mək'flaɪ] **U6**, 60
Meridian Line [məˈrɪdɪən laɪn] **I**
Millennium Dome [mɪleniəm
'dəʊm] **II**
Mr Bean [mɪstə 'biːn] **I**
Nessie ['nesi] **U5**, 46
Notting Hill Carnival [nɒtɪŋ hɪl
'kɑːnɪvl] **U1**, 8
Notting Hill Gate [nɒtɪŋ hɪl
'geɪt] **U1**, 12
Oban Hostel [əʊbn 'hɒstl]
U5, 47
Oxford Circus ['ɒksfəd sɜːkəs]
U1, 12
oznet.au [ɒznet'ɒ] **II**
Paddington Station [pædɪŋtən
'steɪʃn] **U1**, 15
Riverford Farm [rɪvəfɔːd
'fɑːm] **I**
Robbie Williams [rɒbi
'wɪljəmz] **I**
Royal Observatory [rɔɪəl
əb'zɜːvətri] **I**
St Paul's Cathedral [snt'pɔːlz
kə'θiːdrl] **II**
Superman ['suːpəmæn] **U5**, 48
telnet.uk ['telnet juːˈkeɪ] **II**
Thomas Tallis School [tɒməs
tælɪs 'skuːl] **I**
Tillery United [tɪləri juːˈnaɪtɪd]
U3, 32
Tower of London [taʊə əv
'lʌndn] **U1**, 8
Venus Williams [viːnəs
'wɪljəmz] **I**
Waves [weɪvz] **II**
Westlands High School
['westlənds 'haɪ skuːl] **U4**, 38
Westminster [west'mɪntstə]
U1, 15
Will Young [wɪl 'jʌn] **I**
Wimbledon ['wɪmbldn] **I**
With Time [wɪð 'taɪm] **I**
Woodlands ['wʊdləndz] **I**
World Time ['wɜːld taɪm] **I**
X-Boys ['eks bɔɪz] **I**

A

abbiegen turn
Abend evening
  abends in the evening
  am Abend in the evening
  den ganzen Abend lang all evening
  zu Abend essen have dinner
Abendessen dinner
Abenteuer adventure
aber but
abfliegen leave
Abflug departure
abholen fetch; take
Abreise departure
abspülen wash up
abwaschen wash up
Acker field
addieren add
Adresse address
aktiv active
Aktivität activity
alle all
alleine alone
alles all; everything
Alphabet alphabet
als than; when; as
also so
alt old
  Wie alt bist du? How old are you?
am on
  am Abend in the evening
  am Leben sein be alive
  am Morgen in the morning
  am nächsten Morgen the next morning
  am Sonntag on Sunday
  am Wochenende at the weekend
an at; to
anderer/andere/anderes other
anders different
anfangen start
Angst haben be scared
anhaben wear *(Kleidung)*
anhören listen; listen to
anklicken click on
ankommen arrive
Anorak anorak
Anruf phone call
anrufen phone; call
Anrufer/Anruferin caller
anschauen watch; look at
Anschlagtafel board
anschreien shout at
ansehen look at
Ansichtskarte postcard
Antwort answer
antworten answer

Anwesenheitskontrolle registration
Apfel apple
April April
Arbeit job; work
arbeiten work
Arbeitsblatt worksheet
Ärger trouble
Armbanduhr watch
Art style; way
atmen breathe
auch too; also
auf at; on
  auf Englisch in English
  Auf Wiedersehen. Goodbye.
Aufgabe job
aufgeregt upset; nervous; excited
aufhören finish; stop
aufräumen tidy up
aufstehen get up
Auge eye
August August
aus from
  aus ... heraus out of
ausdrucken print out
ausfahren go out
einen Ausflug machen go on a trip
ausgehen go out
ausprobieren try
Grüße ausrichten say hello
ausschalten switch off
außen outside
außerhalb outside
äußerster/äußerste/äußerstes extreme
aussteigen get off
Ausstellung exhibition
Austausch exchange
Auswärtsspiel away game
Auto car

B

Badezimmer bathroom
Bahnhof station
bald soon
Ball ball
Band band
Basketball basketball
Bauernhof farm
Baum tree
beantworten answer
Es ist bedauerlich. It's a pity.
bedeuten mean
beeindruckend awesome
beenden finish
begeistert excited
bei at; with
Bein leg

beinahe almost
beitreten join
bekommen get
belastet stressed
Belastung stress
belegtes Brot sandwich
beliebt popular
bellen bark
benutzen use
beobachten watch
bereits already
Berg mountain
Bergarbeiter/Bergarbeiterin miner
Bericht report
Beruf job
berühmt famous
beschäftigt busy
besichtigen visit
besitzen have got
besonderer/besondere/besonderes special
besorgt worried
besser better
der/die/das beste best
bestellen order
bestürzt upset
Besuch visit
besuchen visit
Bett bed
  ins Bett gehen go to bed
beunruhigt worried
bevor before
bevorzugen prefer
bewölkt cloudy
bezahlen pay
Bibliothek library
Bild picture
billig cheap
bis until
  Bis dann. Speak to you later.
bist are
  Bist du es? Is that you?
  Bist du schon einmal in Deutschland gewesen? Have you ever been to Germany?
bitte please; You're welcome.
blau blue
bleiben stay
Bleistift pencil
Blockflöte recorder
blond blonde
Boot boat
Boy Group boy band
braun brown
brechen break
breit wide
Brief letter
Brieftasche wallet
Brille glasses
bringen take
britisch British

Bruder brother
Buch book
buchen book
Bücherei library
Buchstabe letter
Bude stall
Bulle bull
Bungeespringen bungee
 jumping
Büro office
Bus bus
 mit dem Bus by bus
Busch bush
Butter butter

C

Café café
Cafeteria cafeteria
Camcorder video camera
Campingausflug camping trip
Campingplatz campsite
Campingtrip camping trip
Cartoon cartoon
CD CD
Champion champion
Checkliste checklist
chinesisch Chinese
circa about
Clown clown
Club club
Comicheft comic
Computer computer
cool cool
Cornflakes cornflakes
Couchpotato couch potato
Cousin/Cousine cousin
Curry curry
Currygericht curry

D

da there
 da drin in there
 da hin there
 da ist there is
 da sind there are
Dachboden attic
daheim at home
daher so
Damit basta! That's that!
danach after that
danke (schön) thank you
Danke, gut. Fine, thanks.
dann then
Darts darts
das the; that
 das ist this is
dasselbe the same
dein/deine your

dem that
Demonstration
 demonstration
den that
denken think; believe
 denken an remember
der the; that
derselbe the same
deshalb this is why; so
Detektiv/Detektivin detective
Detektivgeschichte detective
 story
deutsch German
Deutsch German
Deutscher/Deutsche German
Dezember December
Dialog dialogue
Diät diet
dich you
 dich selbst yourself
dick big
die the; that
Dienstag Tuesday
dieser/diese/dieses this
 dies ist this is
diese these
dieselbe the same
Ding thing
dir you
Diskjockey DJ
Disko disco
Diskus discus
diskutieren argue
Donnerstag Thursday
Dorf village
dort there
 dort drin in there
 dort hin there
drangsalieren bully
draußen outside
du you
 du selbst yourself
dunkel dark
durch through
dürfen may
durstig thirsty
DVD DVD
DVD-Spieler DVD player

E

Ei egg
eifersüchtig jealous
eigener/eigene/eigenes own
ein/eine a; an; one
 Einen Moment bitte. Just a
 minute, please.
ein anderer/eine andere/ein
 anderes another
ein paar some
einatmen breathe in

Einband cover
Einbruch break-in
einfach easy
eingeben type in
einige some
einkaufen gehen go shopping
Einladung invitation
einmal once
 einmal pro Woche once a
 week
einpacken pack
einst once
Eintrittskarte ticket
Eis ice cream
Eiscreme ice cream
Eltern parents
E-Mail e-mail
Ende end; ending
enden finish
Engländer/Engländerin
 English
Englisch English
 auf Englisch in English
Ente duck
entlang along
entscheiden decide
Entschuldigung. Excuse me.
entspannen relax
Entwurf design
er he
 er selbst himself
Erbse pea
Erdkunde Geography
Ereignis event
erfahren über find out about
erfinden make up
Ergebnis result
jemanden **erinnern** remind
 somebody
erschüttert shocked
erzählen tell
 erzählen von tell about
es it
 Es ist bedauerlich. It's a pity.
 es gibt there are; there is
 es ist there is
 Es ist schade. It's a pity.
 Es kostet .... It's ....
 es sind there are
essen eat
Essen food; meal
 Essen zum Mitnehmen
 takeaway
Esszimmer dining room
etwas some; something
euch you
euer/eure your
Euro euro
extrem extreme
Extremsport extreme sports

F

fahren go; drive; ride
  mit ... fahren take
Fahrer/Fahrerin driver
Fahrrad bike
Fahrt trip
fair fair
fallen fall
falls if
falsch wrong
Familie family
Fan fan
fantastisch fantastic
Farbe colour
  Welche Farbe hat ... ? What colour is ... ?
fast almost
faul lazy
Februar February
Federmäppchen pencil case
Was **fehlt?** What's missing?
Feld field
Fenster window
Ferien holiday
Ferienwohnung cottage
Fernbedienung remote control
Fernseher TV; television
Fernsehglotzer/Fernsehglotzerin couch potato
Fernsteuerung remote control
fertig ready
Festzug procession
Film film
Filzstift felt-tip
Finale final
finden find; think
Fisch fish pl. fish
fit fit
Fleisch meat
fliegen fly
Flug flight
Flughafen airport
Flugnummer flight number
Flugsteig gate
Flugzeug plane
Fluss river
folgen follow
folglich so
in **Form** fit
Foto photo
  ein Foto machen take a picture
Fotoapparat camera
Fotografie photo
fotografieren take a picture
Frage question
Fragebogen questionnaire
fragen ask
Frau woman pl. women; Mrs (Anrede)

Freak freak
frei free
Freitag Friday
Freizeitzentrum activity centre; leisure centre
fressen eat
Freund boyfriend
Freund/Freundin friend
Freundin girlfriend
frisch fresh
froh happy
Frosch frog
Frucht fruit
Frühling spring
Frühstück breakfast
  zum Frühstück for breakfast
frühstücken have breakfast
Frühstückspension bed and breakfast (B & B)
fühlen feel
Führung tour
Füller pen
funktionieren work
für for
furchtbar awful
Fußball football
füttern feed

G

Gabel fork
Galaxie galaxy
ganz quite
Garten garden
Gast guest
Gaststätte restaurant
geben give
Gebirge mountain
Geburtstag birthday
  Herzlichen Glückwunsch zum Geburtstag! Happy birthday!
Gebüsch bush
gefährlich dangerous
gegen against
gegenüber (von) opposite
Geheimnis secret
gehen go; walk
  Was geht hier vor? What's happening?
  Wie geht's? How are you?
Geist ghost
gelb yellow
Geld money
Gemüse vegetable
genießen enjoy
geöffnet open
Geografie Geography
gerade just
geradeaus straight on
Geräusch noise
gerecht fair

Gern geschehen. You're welcome.
gern haben like
gern mögen love
Geschäft shop
geschehen happen
Geschenk present
Geschichte story; history
geschlossen closed
Gesicht face
Gespräch dialogue
gestern yesterday
  gestern Abend last night
  gestern Nacht last night
gestresst stressed
Getränk drink
Gewinn prize
gewinnen win
gewöhnlich usually
stark **gewürzt** spicy
Gitarre guitar
Glas glass
glauben believe
Glück haben be lucky
glücklich happy
Glückwunsch congratulations
Golf golf
Grad degree
groß big; large; tall
großartig great
Großstadt city
Grube pit
grün green
Gruppe group; band
Gruß greeting
  Grüße ausrichten say hello
gut good; well
  gut aussehend good-looking
  Guten Morgen. Good morning.
  gut in good at
Guthaben credit

H

Haar hair
Haare hair
haben have got; have
Haft detention
Hähnchen chicken
halb (Uhrzeit) half past
Hallo. Hello; Hi.
Haltestelle station
Hand hand
Handy mobile phone; mobile
hart hard
hassen hate
Haus house
  nach Hause home
Hausaufgaben homework
Häuschen cottage

Hausmeister/Hausmeisterin
caretaker
Haustier pet
He! Hey!
Heavy Metal heavy metal
Heft book
Heim home
Heimspiel home game
heiraten marry
heiß hot
heißen mean
Ich heiße .... My name is ....
Wie heißt du? What's your
name?
heiter sunny
helfen help
Hemd shirt
Henne hen
Jetzt aber **her damit**. Just give
it to me.
herausfinden find out
Herbst autumn
Herr Mr *(Anrede)*
herunter down
herunterladen download
heute today
heute Abend tonight
heute Nachmittag this
afternoon
heute Nacht tonight
Hexe witch
hier here
Hier bitte. Here you are.
Hier ist Barbara. It's Barbara.
Hier spricht .... This is ...
speaking.
Hier ist .... This is ...
speaking.
hinauf up
Hindu Hindu
hinduistisch Hindu
hinein into
hineintun put
hinter behind
hinunter down
hinzufügen add
Hit hit
Hobby hobby
hoch high; tall; up
Hochwasser flood
Hochzeit wedding
Hockey hockey
hoffen hope
holen fetch
hören listen to; hear
Hose trousers
Hosentasche pocket
Hotel hotel
hübsch pretty
Hubschrauber helicopter
Huhn hen; chicken
Hülle cover

Hund dog
hundemüde dog-tired
hundert one hundred;
a hundred
hungrig hungry
Hut hat
Hütte cottage

I

ich I; me
ich selbst myself
Ich bin's. It's me.
Ich bin .... I'm ....
Ich heiße .... My name is ....
Ich komme aus .... I'm from ....
Ich möchte .... I'd like to ....
Ich würde gerne .... I'd like
to ....
ideal ideal
Idee idea
ihm him
ihn him
ihnen them
ihr you
ihr/ihre her; their
Ihr/Ihre your
im in
im Internet on the internet
im Zug on the train
Imbiss snack
immer always
in in; at; into
in der Nähe von near
in der Sendung on the
programme
in der Stadt in town
in Form fit
ins Bett gehen go to bed
in Ordnung OK; fine
indisch Indian
Information information
Informationszentrum
Information Centre
Inliner in-line skates
Inline-Skates in-line skates
Instrument instrument
interessant interesting
interessiert sein an be
interested in
Internet internet
im Internet on the internet
Interview interview
**irgendeiner/irgendeine/
irgendein** any
irgendetwas anything
irgendjemand anybody
irgendwelche any
ist is
... ist hinter dir her ... is after
you

J

ja yes; yeah
Jackentasche pocket
Jahr year
Jahrmarkt fair
Januar January
Jazz jazz
Jeans jeans
jeder/jede/jedes every
jeder everybody
jeder (beliebige) anybody
jemals ever
jemand somebody
jemanden erinnern remind
somebody
jemand einen Streich spielen
play a trick on somebody
jene those
jener/jene/jenes that
jetzt now
Jetzt aber her damit. Just give
it to me.
joggen gehen go jogging
Joghurt yoghurt
Journalist/Journalistin
journalist
Jugendherberge youth hostel
Juli July
jung young
Junge boy
Juni June

K

Kaffee coffee
Kaffee trinken have a coffee
kalt cold
Kamera camera
kämpfen fight
Kaninchen rabbit
Kapitel unit
kaputt broken
Karaoke karaoke
Karate karate
Karneval carnival
Karotte carrot
Kartentrick card trick
Kartoffel potato
Käse cheese
Katastrophe disaster
Katze cat
kaufen buy; get
Kebab kebab
kein/keine no; not ... any
keiner nobody
kennen know
kennen lernen meet
Schön dich kennen zu lernen.
Nice to meet you.
Kerker dungeon

Kilometer kilometre
Kinder children
Kinderschminken face painting
Kino cinema
Kirche church
Kiste box
Klasse tutor group; class
  Klasse sieben Year 7
Klassenarbeit test
Klassenzimmer classroom
klassisch classical
Kleid dress
Kleider clothes
Kleidung clothes
klein small
Kleintransporter van
klettern climb
klicken click
klingeln ring
Klingelton ring tone
klug clever
Knopf button
kochen cook
Kohlenbergwerk coal mine
Kohlengrube coal mine
komisch funny
kommen come
  Ich komme aus .... I'm from
  ....
  kommen aus come from
  Woher kommst du? Where
  are you from?
Kommunikation
  communication
König king
Königin queen
können can; may
konnte/konnten could
könnte/könnten could
konnte nicht/konnten nicht
  couldn't
kontrollieren check
Kontrollliste checklist
Konzert concert
koordinieren organize
Kopf head
kosten cost
  Es kostet .... It's ....
  Sie kosten .... They're ....
  Wie viel kosten sie? How
  much are they?
  Wie viel kostet es? How much
  is it?
kostenlos free
krank ill
Krankenpfleger nurse
Krankenschwester nurse
Kredit credit
Kricket cricket
kriegen get
Kriminalbeamter/
  Kriminalbeamtin detective

Kriminalroman detective story
Küche kitchen
Kuchen cake
Küchenschrank cupboard
Kuh cow
Kunst art
kurz short
Küste coast

L

lachen laugh
laden put
Laden shop
Lage situation
Land country
landen land
Landkarte map
landwirtschaftliche Maschine
  farm machine
lang long
langsam slow, slowly
langweilig boring
Laptop laptop
Lärm noise
lassen leave
  lass/lasst uns let's
  Lass mich in Ruhe Leave me
  alone.
Laterne lantern
laufen walk; run
laut loud, loudly
Laut sound
läuten ring
leben live; be alive
am **Leben sein** be alive
legen put
Lego lego
Lehrer/Lehrerin teacher
leicht easy
Tut mir **Leid**. I'm sorry.
Leine line
leise quiet
lernen learn
  lernen über find out about
lesen read
  Noten lesen read music
letzter/letzte/letztes last
Leute people
Lieber/Liebe/Liebes *(in*
  Briefanrede) Dear
Liebe love
lieben love
Lieblings- favourite
Lied song
Liedtext lyrics
Lieferwagen van
Lineal ruler
Linie line
Link link
links left; on the left

Liste list
Löffel spoon
Luft air
Luftballon balloon
lustig funny

M

machen do; make
  einen Ausflug machen go on
  a trip
  eine Reise machen go on a
  trip
  ein Foto machen take a
  picture
  macht/machen Spaß is/are
  fun
Mädchen girl
Magazin magazine
Mahlzeit meal
Mai May
Mama mum
man you
manchmal sometimes
Mann man pl. men
Mannschaft team
Markt market
März March
Mathematik Maths
Maus mouse
Mäuse mice
Meerschweinchen guinea pig
mehr more
mein/meine my
meinen think
Meister/Meisterin champion
Menschen people
merkwürdig strange
Messer knife pl. knives
Meter metre
Methode way
mich me
  mich selbst myself
Milch milk
Million million
Mine mine; pit
Minute minute
mir me
Missgeburt freak
mit with
  mit dem Bus by bus
  mit ... zusammen with
Mitnahmerestaurant
  takeaway
mitnehmen take
  Essen zum Mitnehmen
  takeaway
zu **Mittag essen** have lunch
Mittagessen lunch
Mittagspause lunch break
Mitteilung message

Mittwoch Wednesday
Mobiltelefon mobile phone
**Möchtest du ... ?/Möchten
Sie ... ?** Would you like ... ?
Modell model
modern modern
mögen want (to); enjoy; like; fancy
Einen **Moment** bitte. Just a minute, please.
Monat month
Monster monster
Montag Monday
morgen tomorrow
Morgen morning
morgens in the morning
am Morgen in the morning
Guten Morgen. Good morning.
MP3 Player MP3 player
müde tired
Museum museum
Musik music
müssen must; have to
Muster design
Mutter mother

N

nach to; after; past
nach Hause home
nach unten down
Nachbildung model
Nachmittag afternoon
Nachricht message
Nachsitzen detention
nächster/nächste/nächstes next
nächstes Mal next time
Nacht night
nahe near
in der **Nähe von** near
Nahrung food; diet
Name name
nass wet
Nationalität nationality
Natur nature
natürlich of course
Naturwissenschaft Science
neben next to
nehmen take
nein no
nervös nervous
nett nice
Netz web; network
Netzwerk web; network
neu new
nicht not
konnte nicht/konnten nicht couldn't
nicht dürfen mustn't

nicht können can't
nicht mögen hate
nicht werden won't
nichts not ... anything
nie never
niemals never
niemand nobody
noch still; yet
noch einmal again
noch nicht not yet
noch einer/eine/eins another
Norden north
normalerweise usually
Norwegisch Norwegian
Note grade
Noten lesen read music
Notizen notes
Notizen machen take notes
November November
Nudeln pasta
null oh
Nummer number
nun now
nun (ja) well
nur only; just

O

ob if
oberer Teil top
Obst fruit
oder or
offen open
öffnen open
oft often
Oh. Oh.
ohne without
Ohrring earring
OK OK
Oktober October
Oma grandma
Onkel uncle
online online
Opa grandad
Orangensaft orange juice
Orchester orchestra
ordentlich tidy
organisieren organize
Ort place
Osten east

P

packen pack
Palast palace
Papa dad
Park park
Parkplatz car park
Partner partner
Party party

eine Party feiern have a party
passieren happen
Pause break
peinlich embarrassing
peinlicher more embarrassing
der/die/das **peinlichste** the most embarrassing
Pence *(britische Währungsein-heit)* penny pl. pence
Person person
Pfad path
Pfund *(britische Währungsein-heit)* pound
Pilot/Pilotin pilot
pink pink
Pizza pizza
Plan plan
planen plan
Plappermaul chatterbox
Platz place; position
plötzlich suddenly
Polizei police pl. police
Polizist/Polizistin police officer
Pommes frites chips
Pony pony
Popkonzert pop concert
Popstar pop star
populär popular
Porträt profile
Posaune trombone
Position position
Postamt post office
Poster poster
Postkarte postcard
Präsentation presentation
präsentieren present
Preis prize
prima cool
Prinzessin princess
privat private
pro per
Problem problem
Profil profile
Programm plan
Projekt project
Projekttag project day
Prozent percent
prüfen check
Publikumssport spectator sport
Punkt point
Puzzle jigsaw puzzle

Q

Quiz quiz

R

Radiergummi rubber

Radio radio
Ratschlag tip
Rätsel puzzle
Raum room
Rechnung bill
Recht haben be right
rechts right; on the right
Rechtschreibung spelling
reden talk
 reden mit talk to
 reden über talk about
Regel rule
Regen rain
regnen rain
regnerisch rainy
Reihenfolge order
Reis rice
Reise trip
 eine Reise machen go on a
 trip
reiten ride
Rektor/Rektorin headteacher
rennen run
Rennen race
reparieren repair
Reporter/Reporterin reporter
Restaurant restaurant
Resultat result
retten save
richtig right
riesig large
Roboter robot
Rock skirt
rosa pink
rot red
Route route
Rucksack rucksack
Ruderclub rowing club
rudern gehen go rowing
rufen call; shout
ruhig quiet

S

Sache thing
sagen say; tell
Salat salad
Samstag Saturday
Sandwich sandwich
Sänger/Sängerin singer
Sanktion sanction
Satz sentence
sauber tidy
Schach chess
Schachtel box
Es ist **schade**. It's a pity.
Schaf sheep pl. sheep
Schaltfläche button
scharf spicy
schauen look
schenken give

scheußlich awful
schicken send
schieben push
schießen kick
Schiff boat; ship
Schild sign
schlafen sleep
 schlafen gehen go to bed
Schlafsack sleeping bag
Schlafzimmer bedroom
Schlagzeile headline
Schlagzeug drums
schlecht bad
schlechter worse
der/die/das **schlechteste** the
 worst
schließen close
schlimm bad
schlimmer worse
der/die/das **schlimmste** the
 worst
schlittschuhlaufen gehen go
 ice skating
Schloss castle
Schluss end; ending
 Schluss machen break up
schmerzen hurt
schmerzlich sad
Schnee snow
schnell quick; fast
schockiert shocked
Schokolade chocolate
schön nice
 Schön dich kennen zu lernen.
 Nice to meet you.
schon yet; already
schottisch Scottish
Schrank cupboard
schreiben write
 Schreib zurück (SZ). Text me
 back.
 eine SMS schreiben text
schreien shout; scream
Schritt step
Schuh shoe
Schule school
Schüler/Schülerin pupil
Schulfach subject
Schulfest fair
Schulklasse class
Schulleiter/Schulleiterin
 headteacher
Schulmannschaft school team
Schulstunde lesson
Schuppen shed
Schwamm sponge
schwarz black
 schwarzes Brett board
Schwein pig
Schwester sister
schwierig hard; difficult
Schwierigkeiten trouble

Schwimmbad swimming pool
Schwimmbecken swimming
 pool
schwimmen swim
 schwimmen gehen go
 swimming
Schwimmer/Schwimmerin
 swimmer
See lake
sehen see; look
 Wir sehen uns dort. See you
 there.
Sehenswürdigkeit sight
sehr very
seid are
Seil line
sein be
 Sei/Seid leise. Be quiet.
sein/seine his
Seite page
selbst herself; himself;
 themselves; myself;
 ourselves; yourself
selbstverständlich of course
seltsam strange
Semester term
senden send
Sendung programme
 in der Sendung on the
 programme
September September
setzen put
sich anschließen join
sich ausdenken make up
sich beruhigen relax
sich erinnern remember
sich fühlen feel
sich interessieren für be
 interested in
sich prügeln fight
sich selbst herself; himself;
 themselves
sich treffen meet
sich trennen split; break up
sich verlaufen get lost
sicher sure
sie she; they; them; her
 Sie kosten ... . They're ... .
 sie selbst herself; themselves
Simulator simulator
sind are
singen sing
Situation situation
sitzen sit
Skateboard skateboard
Ski ski
SMS text message
 eine SMS schreiben text
Snack snack
so so
soeben just
Sofa sofa

Sohn son
sollte besser/sollten besser
  ought to
sollte/sollten should
  du solltest you should
Sommer summer
sonderbar strange
sonnig sunny
Sonntag Sunday
  sonntags on Sunday
  am Sonntag on Sunday
Sonst noch etwas? Anything
  else?
sorgfältig careful
Viel **Spaß!** Have fun!
spät late
Speicher attic
Spiel game; play
spielen play
  spielen (eine Rolle) act
  jemand einen Streich spielen
  play a trick on somebody
Spieler/Spielerin player
Spinne spider
Spitze top
Sport sports
Sport(arten) treiben do sports
Sportplatz sports field
Sportunterricht PE
Sprache language
Sprachmittlung mediation
sprechen speak; talk
  sprechen mit talk to
  sprechen über talk about
Sprecher speaker
springen jump
Sprungschanze ski jump
Staatsangehörigkeit
  nationality
Stadt town; city
  in der Stadt in town
Stadtplan map
Stadtzentrum town centre
Stand stall
Star star
stark gewürzt spicy
stecken put
stehen stand
stehlen steal
Stelle place
stellen put
sterben die
Stern star
Stier bull
Stil style
Stimme voice
stinkend smelly
stoßen push
Strafe sanction
Strand beach
Straße road; street
Strecke route

jemand einen **Streich spielen**
  play a trick on somebody
streiten argue
streng strict
Stress stress
Strichmännchen matchstick
  man
Stuhl chair
Stunde hour
Stundenplan timetable
Sturm storm
suchen look for
Süden south
Südwest- southwest
südwestlich southwest
super awesome
surfen surf
  surfen gehen go surfing
Surfen surfing
süß cute
Sweatshirt sweatshirt

T

Tafel board
Tag day
Tal valley
tanzen dance
Tänzer/Tänzerin dancer
Tasche bag
Taschenlampe torch
Tasse cup
Tätigkeit activity
tauschen exchange
tausend one thousand
Taxi taxi
Team team
Tee tea
Teich pond
Teigwaren pasta
Teil part
teilnehmen an take part in
Telefon telephone; phone
Telefongespräch phone call
Telefonzelle phone box
Tempel temple
Temperatur temperature
Tennis tennis
Test test
teuer expensive
Text text
Theaterstück play
Thema topic
Ticket ticket
Tier animal
Tipp tip
Tisch table
Titel title
Titelseite cover
Toast(brot) toast
Tochter daughter

Toilette toilet
toll fantastic
Ton sound
Tor gate
Tornado tornado
tot dead
total totally
Tour tour
Tourist/Touristin tourist
tragen carry; wear *(Kleidung)*
Trainer coach
trainieren train
Training training
Traktor tractor
traurig sad
treffen meet
Treffpunkt meeting place
Treppe stairs
treten kick
Trick trick
Trimester term
trinken drink
Trompete trumpet
T-Shirt T-shirt
tun do; make
Tunnel tunnel
Tür door
Turm tower
Turnhalle sports hall
Turnier competition
Turnschuh trainer
Tut mir Leid. I'm sorry.
Typ type
tyrannisieren bully

U

U-Bahn Underground
üben practise
über over; about
übernachten stay
Überschrift title
Überschwemmung flood
Übung exercise
Übungsheft exercise book
Uhr clock
  ... Uhr ... o'clock
  Wie viel Uhr ist es? What time
  is it?
um at
um zu to
Umfrage survey
Umkleideraum changing
  room
umsteigen nach change to
Umzug procession
unangenehm embarrassing
unangenehmer more
  embarrassing
der/die/das **unangenehmste**
  the most embarrassing

und and
Unfall accident
ungefähr about
Ungeheuer monster
Unglück disaster
unglücklich unhappy
Uniform uniform
Unrecht haben be wrong
uns us
  uns selbst ourselves
unser/unsere our
unter under
Unterführung tunnel
unterrichten teach
Unterrichtsstunde lesson
Urlaub holiday

V

Vater father
Vegetarier/Vegetarierin
  vegetarian
vegetarisch vegetarian
verängstigt sein be scared
veranstalten organize
Veranstaltung event
verbinden join
Verbindung link
Verbrecher/Verbrecherin
  criminal
Verein club
verfehlen miss
... verfolgt dich ... is after
  you
vergessen forget
verkaufen sell
verlassen leave
verlieren lose
Verlies dungeon
vermissen miss
verpassen miss
verregnet rainy
verrückt crazy
verschieden different
verschwistert twinned
verstehen understand
versuchen try
verwenden use
Vetter cousin
Videokamera video camera
viel much
  Viel Spaß! Have fun!
viele lots of; many
vielleicht maybe
viertel nach quarter past
Vogel bird
Volksfest carnival
Volleyball volleyball
völlig totally
von from; of; by
  von ... bis from ... to

vor ago; in front of; to
Vordruck form
vorhaben going to
Vormittag morning
vorne at the front
vorsichtig careful
Vorsingen audition
Vorspielen audition
vorstellen present
vorziehen prefer

W

Wachfrau security guard
Wachmann security guard
wahr true
während during
wahrscheinlich probably
Waliser/Waliserin Welsh
walisisch Welsh
Wand wall
wann when
warm warm
warten wait
  warten auf wait for
warum why
was what
  Was fehlt? What's missing?
  Was geht hier vor? What's
  happening?
  Was ist los? What's wrong?;
  What's the matter?
waschen wash
Wasser water
Website website
wechseln exchange
weg away
Weg path; way
wegen about
weglaufen vor run from
wehtun hurt
weil because
weiß white
weitergehen go on
weitermachen go on
Weitsprung long jump
welcher/welche/welches
  what; which
  Welche Farbe hat ...? What
  colour is ...?
wenn when; if
wer who
werden will; going to; get
werfen throw
Westen west
westindisch; Westinder/
  Westinderin West Indian
Wettbewerb competition
Wetter weather
Wettkampf competition
wichtig important

wie like; as; how
  wie viel how much
  Wie alt bist du? How old are
  you?
  Wie geht's? How are you?
  Wie heißt du? What's your
  name?
  Wie ist ...? What's ... like?
  wie viele how many
  Wie viel kosten sie? How
  much are they?
  Wie viel kostet es? How much
  is it?
  Wie viel Uhr ist es? What time
  is it?
wieder again
Wikinger Viking
wild wild
willkommen welcome
Wind wind
Winter winter
wir we; us
  wir selbst ourselves
  Wir sehen uns dort. See you
  there.
wirklich really
wissen know
  wissen von know about
Wissenschaft Science
Witz joke
wo where
Woche week
Wochenende weekend
  am Wochenende at the
  weekend
Woher kommst du? Where
  are you from?
wohin where
wohnen live; stay
Wohnung flat
Wohnzimmer living room
wolkig cloudy
wollen want (to)
Wort word
Wörterbuch dictionary
wütend angry

Y

Yoga yoga

Z

Zahl number
zahlen pay
Zeichen sign
Zeichentrickfilm cartoon
zeichnen draw
zeigen show
Zeile line

Zeit time
  die Zeiten messen take the
  times
Zeitschrift magazine
Zeitung newspaper
Zelt tent
Zeltplatz campsite
zerbrechen break
zerstören destroy
Zeugnis report; profile
ziehen pull
ziemlich quite
Zimmer room

Zimmer mit Frühstück bed
  and breakfast (B & B)
Zoo zoo
zornig angry
zu too; to; about
zu Hause at home
zu spät late
Zucker sugar
zuerst first
Zug train
Zuhause home
zuhören listen
Zukunft future

zuordnen match
zurück back
zusammen together
zusammenpassen go
  together
  zusammenpassen mit go with
Zusatz extra
zusätzlich extra
Zuschauer/Zuschauerin
  spectator
zusehen watch
zwischen between

Check the answers!

Revision 1-4

1 Questions and answers
2. I could show you the London Eye.
3. No, you ought to wear nice clothes. 4. You can take the Underground. 5. No, I haven't. My old one is OK. 6. I'm not sure. I'll ask my mum first. 7. I went shopping and forgot to call you. 8. Let's meet in the new café. It's cool!

2 Good tips
1. mustn't 2. ought to 3. mustn't
4. must 5. ought to 6. must
7. mustn't 8. ought to

3 Did you forget …?
A: Did you forget our meeting yesterday?
B: Yes, I did. I'm sorry.
A: Where were you?
B: I was at the market.
A: Did you like it? Did you buy anything?
B: It was very cool. I bought a nice present for a friend.
A: What? I don't want to see you again.
B: I'm sorry! Let's talk about it tomorrow.
A: Goodbye!
B: Goodbye.

4 The wrong word
1. driver 2. France 3. listen to it
4. awful 5. message 6. topic

5 How can you do it?
b) 1. run: well, quickly, angrily, …
   2. dance: well, happily, crazily, …
   3. shout: loudly, angrily, …
   4. draw: nicely, beautifully, slowly, …
   5. eat: quickly, slowly, …
   6. sing: loudly, well, quietly, …
   7. play the guitar: nicely, badly, loudly, …
   8. play football: well, badly, quickly, happily, …

Revision 5-8

1 Questions and answers
2. You can take a flight. 3. We'd like to climb Ben Nevis. 4. We'd like to stay in a cottage. 5. Yes, we went there last year. 6. I totally love DJ Dan! 7. If it's sunny, we'll go swimming. 8. Well, I like darts.

2 We haven't done it yet!
2. Tom hasn't been to London yet.
3. Look, I've found some money in the street. 4. Sorry, I've just broken Grandma's expensive cup. 5. We haven't seen Nessie yet. 6. Sorry, I haven't done my homework yet.

3 Myself, yourself, …
2. myself 3. herself, himself
4. themselves 5. ourselves
6. yourselves

4 If …
2. If it's sunny tomorrow, we'll go swimming. 3. But if it rains, we won't go to the beach. 4. If Tom doesn't train more, he'll lose the next race, too. 5. If you don't visit us this evening, I won't see you again before the holidays.

5 Peter Robbins
play, orchestra, practise, loudly, nervous, singer, voice, meet, listen to, download, internet, understands, important, song

6 Andrew
a) Andrew always watches Formula One races on TV. They are really exciting, but also very dangerous.

7 What is it?
Beispiellösungen:
2. This means that you take things from the internet. 3. This is somebody that is not very active. 4. This is the Scottish word for lake. 5. This is a place where you can stay. 6. With a trombone you can make music. 7. You can see this in winter. It's cold and white.

Irregular verbs

Diese Liste enthält alle unregelmäßigen Verben, die in Let's go *vorkommen. Sie enthält jeweils alle drei Formen, auch wenn sie nicht alle im Text erscheinen.*

Verb	Vergangenheit	Perfekt	Auf Deutsch
be	was, were	been	*sein*
break	broke	broken	*(zer)brechen*
buy	bought	bought	*kaufen*
come	came	come	*kommen*
cost	cost	cost	*kosten*
do	did	done	*tun, machen*
draw	drew	drawn	*zeichnen*
drink	drank	drunk	*trinken*
drive	drove	driven	*fahren*
eat	ate	eaten	*essen*
fall	fell	fallen	*fallen*
feed	fed	fed	*füttern*
feel	felt	felt	*(sich) fühlen*
fight	fought	fought	*kämpfen*
find	found	found	*finden*
fly	flew	flown	*fliegen*
forget	forgot	forgotten	*vergessen*
get	got	got	*bekommen, werden*
give	gave	given	*geben*
go	went	gone	*gehen, fahren*
have	had	had	*haben*
hear	heard	heard	*hören*
hurt	hurt	hurt	*wehtun, schmerzen*
know	knew	known	*kennen, wissen*
leave	left	left	*(ver)lassen*
lose	lost	lost	*verlieren*
make	made	made	*machen, tun*
mean	meant	meant	*bedeuten*
meet	met	met	*(sich) treffen*
pay	paid	paid	*(be)zahlen*
put	put	put	*stellen, legen, setzen*
read	read	read	*lesen*
ride	rode	ridden	*reiten, fahren*
ring	rang	rung	*klingeln, anrufen*
run	ran	run	*rennen, laufen*
say	said	said	*sagen*
see	saw	seen	*sehen*
sell	sold	sold	*verkaufen*
send	sent	sent	*schicken*
sing	sang	sung	*singen*
sit	sat	sat	*sitzen*
sleep	slept	slept	*schlafen*
speak	spoke	spoken	*sprechen*
split	split	split	*sich trennen*
stand	stood	stood	*stehen*

Verb	Vergangenheit	Perfekt	Auf Deutsch
steal	stole	stolen	*stehlen*
swim	swam	swum	*schwimmen*
take	took	taken	*bringen, nehmen*
teach	taught	taught	*unterrichten*
tell	told	told	*sagen, erzählen*
think	thought	thought	*denken*
throw	threw	thrown	*werfen*
understand	understood	understood	*verstehen*
wear	wore	worn	*tragen, anhaben*
win	won	won	*gewinnen*
write	wrote	written	*schreiben*

Numbers

0	= nought, zero	20	= twenty
1	= one	21	= twenty-one
2	= two	22	= twenty-two
3	= three	30	= thirty
4	= four	40	= forty
5	= five	50	= fifty
6	= six	60	= sixty
7	= seven	70	= seventy
8	= eight	80	= eighty
9	= nine	90	= ninety
10	= ten	100	= one/a hundred
11	= eleven	101	= one/a hundred **and** one
12	= twelve	202	= two hundred **and** two
13	= thirteen	303	= three hundred **and** three
14	= fourteen	1,000	= one/a thousand
15	= fifteen	1,004	= one/a thousand **and** four
16	= sixteen	2,000	= two thousand
17	= seventeen	2,005	= two thousand **and** five
18	= eighteen	3,500	= three thousand five hundred
19	= nineteen	1,000,000	= one million

In the classroom

Dies ist eine Liste der wichtigsten Arbeitsanweisungen in Let's go.
Deine Lehrerin oder dein Lehrer benutzt sie, wenn du etwas tun sollst:

Act the dialogue with a partner.	*Spiele das Gespräch mit einem Partner.*
Answer the questions.	*Beantworte die Fragen.*
Ask a friend / a partner.	*Frage einen Freund/einen Partner.*
Can you find the numbers?	*Kannst du die Zahlen finden?*
Come to the board, please.	*Komm bitte an die Tafel.*
Go on, please.	*Mach bitte weiter.*
Is that right?	*Ist das richtig?*
Listen and speak.	*Höre zu und sprich nach.*
Look at the pictures.	*Schau dir die Bilder an.*
Listen carefully to the dialogues.	*Höre dir die Dialoge genau an.*
Make a word web.	*Mache ein Wortnetz.*
Make dialogues with a partner.	*Mache Dialoge mit einem Partner.*
Match the names with the dates.	*Ordne die Namen den Daten zu.*
Match the parts of the sentences.	*Ordne die Satzteile einander zu.*
Open your books at page 15.	*Schlagt eure Bücher auf Seite 15 auf.*
Put the words in different groups.	*Ordne die Wörter verschiedenen Gruppen zu.*
Read the sentences.	*Lies die Sätze.*
Right or wrong?	*Richtig oder falsch?*
Say it in English.	*Sag es auf Englisch.*
Take notes.	*Mache dir Notizen.*
Think of something new.	*Denk dir etwas Neues aus.*
What can you see in the picture?	*Was siehst du auf dem Bild?*
What colour is it?	*Welche Farbe hat er/sie/es?*
What's missing?	*Was fehlt?*
What's the right order?	*Was ist die richtige Reihenfolge?*
What's the right word?	*Was ist das richtige Wort?*
Who is it?	*Wer ist es?*
Work in groups and do a presentation.	*Arbeitet in Gruppen und erstellt eine Präsentation.*
Write a short text in English.	*Schreibe einen kurzen Text auf Englisch.*

Das kannst du sagen, wenn du etwas tun möchtest oder ein Problem hast:

Can I go outside, please?	*Darf ich bitte hinausgehen?*
Can I go to the toilet, please?	*Kann ich bitte auf die Toilette gehen?*
Can I open the window, please?	*Kann ich bitte das Fenster aufmachen?*
Can I work with …?	*Kann ich mit … zusammenarbeiten?*
Can we sing a song/play a game?	*Können wir ein Lied singen/ein Spiel machen?*
Can you help me, please?	*Können Sie/Kannst du mir bitte helfen?*
I don't understand this.	*Ich verstehe das hier nicht.*
Pardon?	*Wie bitte?*
Sorry, I haven't got my homework.	*Entschuldigung, ich habe meine Hausaufgaben nicht.*
What's that in German?	*Wie heißt das auf Deutsch?*

Das kannst du sagen, wenn du mit dem Computer arbeitest:

Have you got an e-mail address?	*Hast du eine E-Mail-Adresse?*
What's the address of this website?	*Wie ist die Adresse dieser Webseite?*
Click on this link here.	*Klicke diesen Link an.*
How can I surf the internet?	*Wie kann ich im Internet surfen?*
I can't understand this message.	*Ich verstehe diese Nachricht nicht.*
It won't accept my username/password.	*Mein Benutzername/Passwort wird nicht akzeptiert.*
Can I download it/print it out?	*Kann ich es herunterladen/ausdrucken?*
How can I burn it onto a CD?	*Wie kann ich es auf CD brennen?*
My computer has crashed.	*Mein Computer ist abgestürzt.*
What do I type in here?	*Was muss ich hier eingeben?*

Quellen

Bildquellen:
Umschlag: 1: Mauritius (Merten), Mittenwald; S. 2: Avenue Images GmbH (Stockbyte Gold), Hamburg; U2.1: London Transport Museum, London; S. 3.1: mecom (ddp / Gerhard Blank), Hamburg; S. 8.1: www.britainonview.com, London; S. 8.2: Klett-Archiv (Hacker), Stuttgart; S. 8.3: Mauritius (age), Mittenwald; S. 9.1: Picture-Alliance, Frankfurt; S. 9.2: Corbis (Kim Sayer), Düsseldorf; S. 11.1: Klett-Archiv (Hacker), Stuttgart; S. 15.1: NewsCast, London; S. 17.1: CartoonStock (Mike Mittelstadt), Bath; S. 20.1: Picture-Alliance (Heiko Wolfraum), Frankfurt; S. 20.2: Getty Images (taxi / Erin Patrice O'Brien), München; S. 21.1: Mauritius (A. Mayer), Mittenwald; S. 21.2: Klett-Archiv (Hacker), Stuttgart; S. 21.3: Getty Images (taxi / Denis Felix), München; S. 21.4: Picture-Alliance (Frank May), Frankfurt; S. 22.1: Siemens AG, München; S. 23.1: Getty Images (Photodisc), München; S. 23.2: Avenue Images GmbH (image 100), Hamburg; S. 23.3: Avenue Images GmbH (Digital Vision), Hamburg; S. 23.4: Bananastock RF, Watlington / Oxon; S. 24.1: Klett-Archiv (Fletcher), Stuttgart; S. 24.2: Modular (Steinle), Stuttgart; S. 25.1: Argum (Christian Lehsten), München; S. 26.1: Picture-Alliance (ZB), Frankfurt; S. 26.2: Alamy Images RM (Jeff Morgan), Abingdon, Oxon; S. 27.1: Corel Corporation, Ottawa, Ontario; S. 27.2: Alamy Images RM (Photolibrary Wales), Abingdon, Oxon; S. 27.3: Alamy Images RM (Photolibrary Wales), Abingdon, Oxon; S. 27.4: Avenue Images GmbH (Comstock RF), Hamburg; S. 31.1: Avenue Images GmbH (Brand X RF), Hamburg; S. 35.1: CartoonStock (Geoff McNeill), Bath; S. 35.2: Corbis GmbH (Mark E. Gibson); S. 35.3: Klett-Archiv (Fletcher), Stuttgart; S. 35.4: Fotosearch RF (Design Pics), Waukesha, WI; S. 35.5: Fotosearch RF (Stockbyte), Waukesha, WI; S. 35.6: Alamy Images RM (Jeff Morgan), Abingdon, Oxon; S. 35.7: Getty Images (Image Bank / Alan Thor), München; S. 38.1: Avenue Images GmbH (RF Design Pics), Hamburg; S. 38.2: Alamy Images RM (Photofusion Picture Library), Abingdon, Oxon; S. 39.1: Alamy Images RM (Diomedia), Abingdon, Oxon; S. 40.1: Avenue Images GmbH (RF Design Pics), Hamburg; S. 40.2: Alamy Images RM (Janine Wiedel Photolibrary), Abingdon, Oxon; S. 42.1: Avenue Images GmbH (Image Source), Hamburg; S. 42.2: Avenue Images GmbH (Comstock), Hamburg; S. 46.1: MEV, Augsburg; S. 46.2: Mauritius (Vidler), Mittenwald; S. 46.3: Avenue Images GmbH (image 100), Hamburg; S. 46.4: Alamy Images RM (Photolibrary Wales), Abingdon, Oxon; S. 47.1: Alamy Images RM (colinspics), Abingdon, Oxon; S. 47.2: Alamy Images RM (Photofusion Picture Library), Abingdon, Oxon; S. 47.3: Alamy Images RM (worldthroughthelens), Abingdon, Oxon; S. 52.1: Getty Images (Tony Feder), München; S. 55.1: Alamy Images RM (nagelestock.com), Abingdon, Oxon; S. 58.1: Picture-Alliance (Landov Robert E. Klein), Frankfurt; S. 58.2: Imageshop RF (RF), Düsseldorf; S. 58.3: Picture-Alliance (Yui Mok), Frankfurt; S. 58.4: Fotosearch RF (Brand X Pictures), Waukesha, WI; S. 59.1: Alamy Images Limited (Steve Skjold); S. 59.2: Getty Images (Digital Vision), München; S. 60.1: Corbis (Rune Hellestadt), Düsseldorf; S. 63.1: Fotosearch RF (PhotoDisc), Waukesha, WI; S. 63.2: Fotosearch / Photodisc; S. 63.3: Fotosearch RF (Image 100), Waukesha, WI; S. 64.1: Getty Images (Bruno Vincent), München; S. 64.2: Picture-Alliance (Parsons), Frankfurt; S. 64.3: Schlüter, Heinz, Flensburg; S. 64.4: Corbis (George Hall), Düsseldorf; S. 65.1: Avenue Images GmbH (Digital Vision RF), Hamburg; S. 65.2: Getty Images (Graeme Robertson), München; S. 65.3: Picture-Alliance (Steve Pope), Frankfurt; S. 67.1: Getty Images (stone / Jorn Georg Tornter), München; S. 67.2: Picture-Alliance (Barry Batcher), Frankfurt; S. 71.1: www.jalite.co.uk; S. 73.1: CartoonStock (Robert Thompson), Bath; S. 76.1: Bananastock RF (RF), Watlington / Oxon; S. 76.2: Alamy Images RM (Profimedia.CZ s.r.o.), Abingdon, Oxon; S. 76.3: Getty Images (PhotoDisc), München; S. 76.4: Getty Images (Image Bank / Terje Rakke), München; S. 76.5: Getty Images (Workbook Stock / Mills), München; S. 77.1: Alamy Images RM (Photo Network), Abingdon, Oxon; S. 77.2: Avenue Images GmbH (Rubberball RF), Hamburg; S. 77.3: MEV, Augsburg; S. 77.4: www.britainonview.com, London W6 9EL; S. 80.1: Alamy Images RM (Lisa Battaglene), Abingdon, Oxon; S. 81.1: Klett-Archiv (Smith), Stuttgart; S. 84.1: Getty Images (Photodisc), München; S. 84.2: Alamy Images RM (Alex Segre), Abingdon, Oxon; S. 88.1: Klett-Archiv (Smith), Stuttgart; S. 88.2: Klett-Archiv (Smith), Stuttgart; S. 88.3: Klett-Archiv (Smith), Stuttgart; S. 8.4: Klett-Archiv (Smith), Stuttgart; S. 88.5: Klett-Archiv (Smith), Stuttgart; S. 88.6: Klett-Archiv (Smith), Stuttgart; S. 88.7: Klett-Archiv (Smith), Stuttgart; S. 88.8: Klett-Archiv (Smith), Stuttgart; S. 88.9: Klett-Archiv (Smith), Stuttgart; S. 88.10: Alamy Images RM (oote boe), Abingdon, Oxon; S. 89.1: Klett-Archiv (Smith), Stuttgart; S. 89.2: Klett-Archiv (Smith), Stuttgart; S. 89.3: Corbis (David Ball), Düsseldorf; S. 89.3: Klett-Archiv (Smith), Stuttgart; S. 90.1: Corbis (Roy McMahon), Düsseldorf; S. 90.2: Getty Images (PhotoDisc), München; S. 90.3: MEV, Augsburg

Textquellen:
S. 23: © Happy Mel Boopy's Cocktail Lounge And Music / Zomba Songs Inc., Musik-Edition Discoton GmbH (BMG Music Publ. Germany) München, Ooky Spinalton Music / EMI April Music Inc., EMI Music Publishing Germany GmbH & Co. KG, Hamburg; S. 61: © EMI Music Publishing Germany GmbH & Co KG, Hamburg, Universal Music Publ. GmbH, Berlin; S. 79: © Queen Music Ltd. D / A / CH / Osteuropäische Länder: EMI Music Publishing Germany GmbH, Hamburg; S. 90.1: © 2001 by Kenn Nesbitt. Reprinted from *The Aliens Have Landed!* with permission from Meadowbrook Press; S. 90.2: © 2004 by Matthew M. Fredericks. Reprinted from *If Kids Ruled the School* with permission from Meadowbrook Press

Flags

Match the flags with the countries. You can find the answers on the internet.